Praise for *Crystal Skulls*

This is a book on crystal skulls I would absolutely buy—which is unusual for me as I find most books out on the skulls either too strange or too dry.

—Edwin Courtney, skullkeeper,
spiritual teacher, and channel

Wow. That's a slow, stopped-in-the-tracks and reverential wow, the wow of someone who really enjoyed the opening of this book, recognizing quite how special the subject is. It ticked the boxes for me—informative, fun, enticing. I simply hadn't anticipated the solidity, the depth of the crystal—not to mention colour, pattern, chaos, order . . . Please pass on my apologies to Horace, I underestimated him in my imagination!

—Richard Bryson

As a relative newcomer to the world of crystal skulls, I found this book a fascinating mix of a walk through history with really workable and easy-to-understand suggestions on how to start to work with them. It is an extremely good read. I thoroughly recommend it.

—Stephen Chapman, President,
College of Psychic Studies, London

Crystal Skulls

CRYSTAL SKULLS

Ancient Tools for Peace, Knowledge, and Enlightenment

JUDY HALL

WEISER BOOKS

This edition first published in 2016 by
Weiser Books, an imprint of
Red Wheel/Weiser, LLC
With offices at:
65 Parker Street, Suite 7
Newburyport, MA 01950
www.redwheelweiser.com

ISBN 978-1-57863-594-8

Library of Congress Cataloging-in-Publication Data
available upon request

Cover design by Jim Warner
Cover photograph © Science Photo Library / SuperStock
Interior by Jane Hagaman
Typeset in ITC New Baskerville and Chantilly

Printed in the USA
IBI

Dedication

My deepest love and thanks go to skullkeeper Edwin Courtney, not only for his friendship and support over many years, but also for so generously sharing information with me. You are a one-off, Edwin, and I treasure you!

Disclaimer

No medical claims are made for stones in this book and the information is not intended to act as a substitute for medical treatment. Healing properties are given for guidance only and are, for the most part, based on anecdotal evidence and/or traditional therapeutic use. Illness is a dis-ease, the final manifestation of spiritual, environmental, psychological, karmic, emotional, or mental imbalance or distress. Healing means bringing mind, body, and spirit back into balance and facilitating evolution for the soul. It does not imply a cure.

Contents

Acknowledgments

My deepest love and gratitude goes to all the skullkeepers, carvers, and others who have so willingly shared their knowledge and experience with me, sometimes in the midst of profound life changes and the darkest of times. Being a skullkeeper isn't all sweetness and light, so I thank you all from the bottom of my heart. Every effort was made to trace holders of what might be copyrighted material referred to in the book. Some skullkeepers proved particularly elusive. The Internet obviously isn't as effective as the crystalline net in communicating! So my thanks in absentia to all those from whom it was not possible to obtain consent. References have been given wherever possible, but occasionally the primary source was impossible to determine.

Special thanks, too, to my crystal group, who take the time for new adventures with me every month. Without you I would know less of crystal qualities and of sharing without limits. My love to you all and my heartfelt thanks for your contributions, whether in the book or not.

And last but certainly not least, to Terrie Birch who has joined me on so many healings adventures and to the crystal skulls and skull beings for their wisdom, care, and inspiration, my love and thanks.

Introducing the Crystal Skulls

Crystal skulls are a conundrum. The skulls are here to bring peace and knowledge, so they tell us. They seek to awaken higher consciousness in humanity. To offer healing to the Earth. But they have stirred up vigorous controversy. There is little authentic empirical evidence as to their origins. Some of the well-known skulls, such as the Mitchell-Hedges and "Max," are said to be exceedingly ancient. Modern technology is, however, showing that virtually all crystal skulls are comparatively recent, although, of course, the material from which they are carved—throughout this book generally referred to as "crystal"—*is* exceedingly ancient.

When it comes to crystal skulls, we need to ask if there are just too many caveats for them to be credible. Although, given that it is postulated that a separate "higher consciousness" animates the skull, we could ask whether it really matters how old they are. What about the hundreds of contemporary skulls sold around the world? Are these a cynical marketing ploy as claimed by skeptics? Or is something extraordinary going on?

Fact or Fiction?

In the chapters that follow, we'll explore how a crystal skull might enlighten and enliven your life. First, we'll look at questions that the skulls invoke. Sifting fact from fable is a major challenge. So much is presented as certainty when it is anything but. It is virtually impossible to consult primary source material. Hearsay is

Merit-Aten. The author's Egyptian Sodalite head. Not all skulls are clear crystal. (*Courtesy of Sandra Birch, www.ksc.crystals.com*)

rife, especially online, but print authors are equally culpable. Speculation is dressed as fact, and fabrications and deceptions abound, deliberately or otherwise. Stories are passed around, and get embroidered in the telling. Without provenance and documented archaeological context, there is no certitude. But, as has been said, absence of evidence is not evidence of absence. Who knows what a validated archaeological dig may soon reveal?

In talking about crystal skulls, departures from "truth" inevitably occur. But what is truth? Just because the origins of a skull are dubious does not invalidate people's subsequent experiences.

First, I'd like to share with you how I was beguiled by a skull. I'll also take the opportunity to introduce a rather idiosyncratic—and somewhat anarchic—character: Horace, my Smoky Quartz skull. He appears at intervals throughout this book.

Meeting the Skulls

Have you ever come face-to-face with a skull and had it call to you? I did, in 1975 in the Museum of Mankind (now once again part of the British Museum) in London. The skull was a life-size, flawless crystal with more than a tinge of blue about it (you can see its picture on page xvi). The mesmerizing eyes were alive with intense intelligence. It was a truly awesome experience, like being pulled in by a powerful tractor beam. I gazed into it, watching an ancient South American temple going about its daily busi-

Crystal

Throughout this book, the term "crystal" is used regardless of whether or not the material from which skulls are carved has a crystalline structure or is amorphous, or whether it is precious, semiprecious, or non-precious stone.

Crystal Skull

A crystal skull is carved in the shape of a humanoid, extraterrestrial, or animal skull. Skulls vary in size from a few inches to life-size. Many are clear Quartz crystal, but other types of crystal can be used (see pages 167–180). Throughout this book, the term "skull" refers to a crystal skull unless otherwise stated.

ness. I thought I stood there for a few minutes, but it was almost two hours. I had been seduced.

I'm aware that the British Museum skull has since been deemed "fake" in that it was carved within the last two hundred years, probably in Germany from Brazilian Quartz. That does not negate my experience. Until I read the label on the way out, I had no idea where it was, at the time, thought to have originated. I'd never heard of crystal skulls. *Arthur C. Clarke's Mysterious World,* in which a skull dominated the opening credits, wasn't aired until 1980. *Indiana Jones and the Kingdom of the Crystal Skull* wouldn't appear until 2008. Nothing in my experience or my psyche in the 1970s was attuned to crystal skulls. Elsewhere in the world, however, interest was stirring. So was I picking up on a burgeoning belief system? Reading impressions other people had left in the skull? Frank Dorland would certainly have said so (see page 52). Or was something else entirely going on? Were they calling to me? This

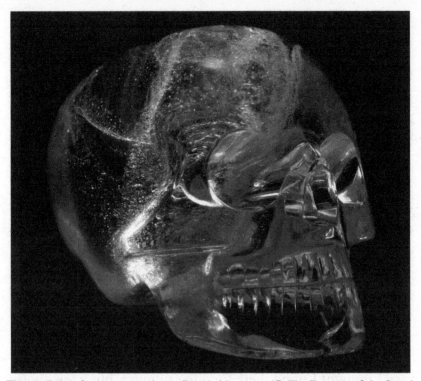

The skull that first entranced me. British Museum. (© *The Trustees of the British Museum. All rights reserved*)

book has been written in part to explore that idea. I invite you to join me in my journey and to experience these enigmatic beings for yourself.

It took another thirty-five years for me to start collecting crystal skulls. I'd met several skulls over the intervening period. Skullkeeper Edwin Courtney introduced me to a small portion of his vast collection and to skull lore. That was in the faded grandeur of a ballroom in a particularly deprived part of the UK. The skulls lifted the gloom, but didn't grab me. It took a visit to Glastonbury, home of all things magical, mystical, and downright weird, to get me hooked.

"Get me out of here," a voice pleaded. The friend I was with said, "I think someone's talking to you." So into the shop we went. I had already voiced the intention of buying a skull. It felt like time. I had in mind a clear crystal like the one I'd seen in the museum. Something light and bright. I had not envisioned this inky black one. Out of the shop with it I came. Once a skull adopts you, it seems you have little choice.

I took the skull home and did extensive clearing on it. Fortunately David Eastoe, founder of Petaltone Essences, created new essences that helped to heal the skull.[1] It had had a hard few months. A murder had been committed in front of it, and it had been living next to the favorite hangout of a group of alcoholics. Their aggressive behavior was the antithesis of the spirituality for which Glastonbury is famed. The darker side of the light.

Initially, the skull seemed to have taken on the boorish characteristics of the addicts. Maybe it thought that was how all humans communicated? Little impact had been made by the people inside the crystal shop. It glowered at me and resisted attempts to interact. I knew there was a crystal being in there that needed my help. I could understand why it was reluctant to fully manifest. Over the next year or so the formerly almost black, impenetrable head gradually lightened and became full of bubbles. It was still a pretty intense, curmudgeonly companion who stood no nonsense, however. I had to remind it that a sense of humor is essential in this world.

This summer I took it to my local sacred site at the solstice. We placed it in bright sunlight with a Golden Healer crystal spiral around it. What a difference that made! The skull lit up like a Christmas tree. The inside of the skull cleared miraculously. So many sparkles, like a glass of champagne. And the rainbows!

It became clear to me that the skull's role is to help with transitions and transmutations, clearing trauma and toxicity, and with earth-healing. I had more communication with it in the next few hours than in all the previous years put together. It's finally given me an everyday name: Horace. The initial one was an impossible tongue twister. So he's mellowing. His innate wisdom is being revealed as more of the higher consciousness within is able to manifest. His story illustrates how skulls may need nurturing and care, especially if they've been traumatized before they reach you. Horace was worth the wait.

Horace awakens. Summer Solstice 2014. The author's Smoky Quartz Earth-healer skull. (*Courtesy of* Terrie Birch, *www.astrologywise.co.uk*)

Shared Experience

This book draws not only on my experience but also that of other people. Just as the skulls themselves share an information field, so crystal skullworkers tune in to an "overall-consciousness" with remarkable congruency. Well-known skullkeepers have volunteered information for this book. So have people who are not in the limelight but are working with the skulls every day—or attuning to them for the first time. Throughout this book you'll find "skulls in action" examples to give you an idea of what you might expect when using a skull. I would emphasize that everyone's experience is a uniquely personal one, however. Your experience may be totally different.

To start with, here's what a member of one of my crystal meditation groups experienced upon meeting Horace. It was midway through his protracted awakening process, when he was still healing.

Skulls in Action: First Encounter

My first meaningful interaction with a crystal skull took place in Judy Hall's dining room during a group meditation. I was holding a fire and ice crystal and just returning from a wonderful healing journey to the heart of Mother Earth. As I opened my eyes, I had the distinct feeling of being watched. A large, smoky quartz skull was sitting looking down at me from the shelf opposite.

He was one of many amongst a collection of crystal skulls, but it really felt as if he was trying to get my attention. I thought I was imagining things, but I kept catching sight of him out of the corner of my eye during the group's discussions. Each time I looked up at the skull, I could have sworn he had moved slightly. Eventually, I realized with a slight chill or was it thrill (!), that he had turned to face me directly, having previously faced at an angle to me and to his left.

I now felt that the skull's energy was increasing as if he was jumping up and down to get my attention. Eventually, I rather tentatively said to Judy that I felt the skull was trying to get my attention and that I was sure he had moved. Judy looked up at him and confirmed, without surprise, that he had moved around. I asked if I could hold him, and it was an extraordinary experience.

The skull craved affection and comfort, and I found myself stroking him and offering him unconditional love as I would to a dog that needed healing and reassurance. I couldn't believe that I felt this way. I had previously avoided skulls in crystal shops, and I had privately wondered why people would want a crystal shaped like a skull. Well now I had my answer, and I was being educated in the fact that crystal skulls have personalities, individual needs and special healing qualities.

I felt great compassion for the skull, and Judy explained that he was still healing from a traumatic past. He had resided in a shop window where he witnessed the worst of human behaviour. He had asked her to rescue him. When he first came home with Judy, the skull had appeared almost black. With love and healing, he was changing colour, lightening and developing rainbows. His eye sockets were still black, speaking volumes about what he had seen. This skull regularly interacts with the meditation group, and it is fascinating to observe how others in the group have deep experiences working with him.

—Susannah Rafaelle
(animal healer and energy worker)

When my crystal group met soon after Horace's summer solstice activation, they commented that he seemed like a different skull both physically, with his translucent bubbly rainbow eyes, and psychologically, with his much improved personality. There are times when it is worth persevering with a skull. At other times, it may be necessary to evict an unwanted presence and invite in a higher one (see pages 105–106).

Using this Book

This book is divided into two parts. Part I is an overview that gives you the who and what of the crystal skulls: what they are, what they communicate, what people say about them, who uses them, and what they can do for you. It navigates a path through the speculation, misinformation, and disinformation that surrounds crystal skulls. Part II is a practical guide that assists you in choosing, tending, and using a crystal skull. It helps you to attune to a skull for personal and planetary healing, consciousness-raising, divination, journeying, and accessing the Akashic Record. Part II also facilitates identifying and building on the modes of perception with which you receive metaphysical communications.

So, if you need information, check out Part I. If you want to get hands-on immediately, go to Part II. If you wish to understand what the different types of skulls and crystal materials offer, that information is also in Part II. The Resources section directs you toward reputable sources for skulls, and the endnotes give you the sources drawn on for this book. There is also a glossary at the end of the book that defines unfamiliar terms.

PART I

What Exactly Are the Crystal Skulls?

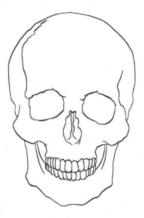

Skulls have taken on an aura of magic and mystery like no other crystal artifact. They excite the imagination and are an amazing tool for personal and planetary evolution if used with right intention and metaphysical awareness.

—Judy Hall, *Crystal Bible: Volume 3*

CHAPTER 1

What Are Crystal Skulls?

Crystal skulls are lifelike or exaggerated carvings in crystal or stone that represent humanoid, animal, bird, or "alien" (I prefer the term "star being") heads. They can best be described as a crystalline interstellar Internet. Many of the older skulls are Quartz, Jade, or Amber, but today skulls can be obtained in almost any material. They are said to access an information field implanted long ago by an advanced consciousness and to function rather like a giant computer memory chip or a phone app. The skulls also link to the Akashic Record, the vast plane of collective memories, potentialities, and possibilities otherwise known as cosmic

Definition: Crystal

Matter exists in three main varieties: the gaseous state, the liquid state, and the solid state. Solid matter, in which the atoms, molecules, or ions are arranged in a regularly repeating pattern throughout, is said to be crystalline; all other solid matter is said to be amorphous (noncrystalline), although the distinction is not always sharp. Practically all metals, minerals, and alloys are crystalline, while glasses, plastics, ceramics, and gels are amorphous. A single piece of crystalline matter is called a crystal. (Encyclopedia Britannica) consciousness. Many of the skulls are believed to house mentors from higher dimensions. This is what one modern skullkeeper has to say: "Crystals can be seen as the most pure form in which consciousness can manifest itself in this reality . . . [Crystal skulls] create together a unique field, that to some degree can be compared to the collective (un)consciousness of mankind."[1]

Why Crystal?

So, why are the skulls carved from crystal? Well, Quartz, as with other materials containing silica, is a highly resonant transceiver. It is capable of storing and retrieving programming as well as gen-

A conclave of skulls
(Courtesy of Jeni Campbell / www.angeladditions.co.uk)

erating energy through piezoelectric and pyroelectric processes. Quartz broadcasts a specific frequency or radio wave (think old crystal radio sets) so that it establishes a rapport with the human mind. Skulls can be regarded as a terminal of an original, in all senses of the word, virtual computer, the type of which scientists to date can only dream. That dream is getting closer, as we'll see.

Crystal Skull Classifications

Ancient peoples were extremely skilled in stone carving, as is demonstrated in museum exhibits around the world. Some had extremely sophisticated techniques for stone working. Seven-thousand-year-old semiprecious Lapis Lazuli beads drilled with holes almost invisible to the naked eye, intricately carved and meticulously polished statues and jewelry, and many other artifacts attest to their mastery. In the "Stone Age" the technology was exactly that. Stone working skills were passed down through the generations. Unfortunately, however, it is impossible to tell exactly how old a carving is, as crystal and stone, unlike wood and other organic substances, cannot be carbon-dated. Nevertheless, there are clues to be found in the tooling and polishing methods used in the carving. Three classifications are commonly used for crystal skulls.

NEW AND CONTEMPORARY

Contemporary skulls are manufactured by carvers in Brazil, North America, China, Germany, and elsewhere from a wide variety of materials. A few are hand carved and beautifully detailed, copied from older artifacts, but most are machine made. They are for sale on eBay or specialist skull websites and in crystal shops around the globe. Modern skulls have machine-tool markings.

OLD (SECOND GENERATION)

Old skulls were created between 100 years and about 1,000 years ago (1000–1900 CE) and are believed to be copies of more archaic skulls. Many are claimed to have been discovered in ancient ruins in Mexico or Central America or brought out of Tibet. Some are reported to have been under the guardianship of hereditary keepers from indigenous people around the world. Old skulls have hand-tool marks, although the younger of these skulls may also have machine-tool marks. They are often small and crudely carved.

ANCIENT (PRIMARY)

Ancient skulls were created from around 1,000–2,000 years ago (1–1000 CE) to way back in the mists of time. Such skulls have no discernible modern tool marks, but exhibit hand-tool marks and polishing methods. Some are claimed to have originated in the antediluvian civilizations of Atlantis and Lemuria or even come from outer space. Several small skulls dating back to the Stone Age, carved from Jade or Amber, have apparently been found in China.

Ancient Skulls

The skulls have a long precedent. Mesoamericans as far back as the Olmecs (1200–400 BCE) carved huge stone heads and smaller skulls in rock crystal, Quartz, and Jade. Chinese Jade skulls appear to go back as far as the Neolithic era, dating from between 6000 to 4000 BCE. They were also carved in Amber, which was highly prized in the ancient world as a medicine and has an electrostatic charge when rubbed (no wonder it seemed magical to ancient peoples). The Amber was sourced in Burma (Myanmar) and carried along a well-established trade route from the Baltic to the Far East.

Skulls: Many and Varied

Modern crystal skulls come in all shapes and sizes, forms and materials (see the crystal directory page 167–180). Some are anatomically realistic, others delicate and lovely. There are alien, otherworldly, and, to some minds, ugly examples. And the so-called "laughing" or "screaming" skulls. Other skulls take the form of an animal, bird, or mythical creature.

Where Do They Come From?

No one really knows the origins of truly ancient skulls. There is no provenance, no unbroken documented chain of ownership from initial archaeological discovery or demonstrable indigenous use up to the present day. That doesn't stop extravagant claims from being made. The answers given are many and varied. As far as the skulls of antiquity are concerned, they are usually deemed to be a legacy from earlier, more intelligent cultures. Suppositions center around Atlantis and Lemuria, or extraterrestrial civilizations such as in the Pleiades. A typical alien source channeling states:

> The skull . . . was made by humanoids who were not of this Earth. They would be termed Pleiadeans to your knowledge. They extended within another parallel galaxy to your Milky Way as an invisible counterpart of your sixth dimensional existence, like a sister galaxy. The skull was actually brought to the Earth realm fully created. It was teleported along with visitors who came to teach Earth mortals about their Pleiadean heritage . . . expanding mortal awareness of physical life in order to regain understanding of relationship with light-and-sound life forces inherent within the realm.[2]

Another theory suggests that the skulls were left behind by a subterranean race that lived, or still lives, within a Hollow Earth, with all the attendant mythology that conjures. For the most part, the older crystal skulls, as opposed to stone heads, are reputed to have been found in China, the Himalayas, and Central and South America. One of the most often suggested sources for the archaic skulls is the Mayan civilization, but as has been pointed out by the British Museum:

> Skull imagery figures prominently in Aztec art and religious symbols, and not in that of the Mayans. The Aztecs were also more highly skilled in sculpting with crystal. It could be that the skulls found in Mayan ruins

What Exactly Are the Crystal Skulls?   7

are actually displaced Aztec relics . . . or, as some sus-
pect, this incongruity may indicate that some accounts
of the skulls' origins are phony.[3]

So, for the moment, the answer once again is we really don't know.

Male, Female, or Genderless?

I've met both masculine and feminine skulls of all types: humanoid, dragon, and power animal. There is at least one pair of
ancient complementary skulls that fit together to form a beautiful heart shape. Susan Isabelle Boynton, who lives at the foot of
Mount Shasta, is in possession of the pair of skulls. Only one-and-
a-half and two inches long, they form a single "heart-brain," and
extraordinary claims have been made for them. El Aleator and El
Za Ra were found by their keeper in Belize.[4] Some modern skulls
are carved in interlocking pairs as well. I've also come across
skulls that had a more unearthly, neutrally gendered feeling to
them. They would say that their elevated consciousness is beyond
gender as we know it in the same way that they have transcended,
or never known, ego-based personality.

And How Might They Work?

At its simplest, the explanation of how skulls work may come down
to the fact that crystals are composed of atoms that vibrate and
create light and sound. They generate the music of the spheres
for those with ears to hear and an electrical current for those with
the sensitivity to feel. Clues as to how skulls work are also emerging
from the latest scientific and information technology research:

> The crystal cells transmit radio-like waves through
> the nervous system to cortex cells in the . . . brain.
> (There), they are decoded and transformed into
> meaningful signs which can be recognized as images,

words, or perhaps just a feeling of knowledge in the conscious mind. These messages can be received from many sources, but mainly they seem to come from the bank of the subconscious memory and super conscious sources.[5]

We know that information is encoded and retrieved through frequency and vibration. That's the basis of all communication. The exact mechanism for the skulls themselves? Well, the human pineal gland contains "brain sand," Calcite and Fluorapatite crystals.[6] The pineal gland has long been thought to be the metaphysical third eye. Brain sand may well entrain and resonate in harmony with the crystal matrix of the skulls.

One skull researcher, the late "Nick" Nocerino, used light and sound to unlock the codes within the skulls. He discovered, incidentally to his research, that various colors invariably took him back to specific time frames. Other people suggest the information within the skulls takes the form of a deliberately implanted hologram. With a hologram, each tiny part contains the whole. All that is needed is the key to unlock the information. An enlightened quantum scientist will no doubt explain the process one day. For now, we can look at cutting-edge research to open up possible explanations.

Time Out of Mind

It is claimed that the information and codes held by the skulls are exceedingly ancient, originating far back in time. Is this possible? Well, Quartz is a type of silica, and computers run on silicon crystals. Rapid advances are being made in the information storage field using . . . guess what? . . . Quartz. Let's look at some recent scientific headlines:

"Data Saved in Quartz Glass Might Last 300 Million Years"
Scientific American

"Hitachi unveils quartz-based storage,
data may last 100 million years"
www.techspot.com

"Data that lives forever is possible"
www.phys.org

"Data Storage in Crystal Quartz will change Everything!"
www.themindunleashed.org

"5D 'Superman memory crystal' heralds
unlimited lifetime data storage"
Physics World, the member magazine of the Institute of Physics

A groundbreaking glass plate has been making the news because of its apparently limitless capacity to store data *forever.* Hitachi and scientists from Southampton University created a device said to be capable of storing data virtually indefinitely with no degradation. The device is a two-centimeter-wide and two-millimeter-thick glass structure that houses four layers of dots created by a femtosecond laser. The laser produces extremely short pulses of light and implants the information in binary form. It is believed that even in the far future this could be read with a basic optical microscope. Hitachi says, "The medium could be ideal for safekeeping a civilization's most vital information, museum holdings or sacred texts." Exactly what is claimed to be held by the crystal skulls.

In addition, scientists have used Quartz crystals to store data in 5D. Under the headline "Mega Quartz Crystal Storage Drives Will Hold Data Forever" *www.gajitz.com* suggests that "with the invention of the 'Superman memory crystal,' scientists have found a better use for a piece of quartz than the New Age industry. They've created what is seemingly the world's most amazing zip drive." Is it more a case of reinvented rather than "created"?

Did the beings that carved the original crystal skulls understand how to use crystals for data storage?

Did they create the world's first zip drive? One that only needs the power of mind to unlock it rather than an optical microscope or futuristic technology? A zip drive that is embedded within the crystals of our planet? Skullkeepers around the world would answer a resounding Yes!

Skullkeepers would also remind us, however, that the information comes from a higher consciousness that takes over the skull and "decodes" information encoded into the Akashic Record or cosmic consciousness. From there it is downloaded through the skull. Many of the skull carvers state that they are aware of a consciousness activating the skull when they carve the eyes. It may be necessary to invite a higher awareness into a skull in a dedicated activation process (see chapter 11).

The Holy Grail of Computing Science

So, let's take a look at another field that may give us a clue as to how crystal skulls work. The holy grail of computing science is artificial intelligence (AI). The supercomputer is making enormous progress. AI learns from its experiences, constantly updating itself. "Over the past five years, cheap computing, novel algorithms, and mountains of data have enabled new AI-based services that were previously the domain of sci-fi and academic white papers," says Robert McMillan, senior writer for *Wired Magazine*. Under the headline, "The Three Breakthroughs that Have Finally Unleashed AI on the World," Kevin Kelly reports on a rapidly changing industry on *Wired.com*:

> A few months ago I made the trek to the sylvan campus of the IBM research labs in Yorktown Heights, New York, to catch an early glimpse of the fast-arriving, long-overdue future of artificial intelligence . . . The original

Watson is still here—it's about the size of a bedroom, with 10 upright, refrigerator-shaped machines forming the four walls . . . It is surprisingly warm inside, as if the cluster were alive.

Today's Watson is very different. It no longer exists solely within a wall of cabinets but is spread across a cloud of open-standard servers that run several hundred "instances" of the AI at once. Like all things cloudy, Watson is served to simultaneous customers anywhere in the world, who can access it using their phones, their desktops, or their own data servers. This kind of AI can be scaled up or down on demand. Because AI improves as people use it, Watson is always getting smarter; anything it learns in one instance can be immediately transferred to the others. And instead of one single program, it's an aggregation of diverse software engines—its logic-deduction engine and its language-parsing engine might operate on different code, on different chips, in different locations—all cleverly integrated into a unified stream of intelligence . . . Consumers can tap into that always-on intelligence directly, but also through third-party apps that harness the power of this AI cloud . . . Everything that we formerly electrified we will now cognitize. This new utilitarian AI will also augment us individually as people (deepening our memory, speeding our recognition) and collectively as a species. There is almost nothing we can think of that cannot be made new, different, or interesting by infusing it with some extra IQ . . .[7]

That sounds remarkably like the crystalline skulls network to me, with the skulls being the computer terminals, or possibly apps that access the overall information field. The writer ends with a message that could have come straight from the natural intelligence of the skulls themselves: "The greatest benefit of the arrival of artificial intelligence is that AIs will help define humanity. We need AIs to tell us who we are."

Or perhaps the crystal skulls do this for us?

CHAPTER 2

An Artifact with Mystical Powers or an Ingenious Hoax?

Crystal skulls generate more controversy than any other ancient artifact. The subject has spawned an ever-wilder mythology for and against. People feel passionately about these objects, many of which are venerated as wise beings and guardians of humanity. Skullkeepers claim they have healing powers. The keeper of the skull named ET, for instance, believes that it helped to heal her massive brain tumor.[1] People who have encountered well-known skulls describe them as giving off strong psychic energy.

The skulls are most often claimed to be Aztec or Mayan. The British Museum states:

> Human skulls and skull imagery are known to have featured in Aztec iconography in Mexico at the time of first contact with the Spanish in AD 1519. They were worked by Aztec, Mixtec and even Mayan lapidaries. A human skull covered with turquoise and lignite mosaic is displayed in the Mexican gallery (Room 27) of the British Museum. However, they were usually carved in relief in basalt or limestone as architectural elements.[2]

The British Museum's own skull has been shown to be a relatively recent nineteenth-century carving. There may be other genuinely archaic skulls still waiting to be discovered.

The Mitchell-Hedges Skull

The best example of the controversy over crystal skulls is the famous—or infamous, depending on your point of view—skull known as the Mitchell-Hedges. This is the most frequently written about skull. Claimed to be exceedingly old, it has been scientifically tested. It was dismissed as a fake. It has been dubbed "The Skull of Doom," although that title may have been a publicity stunt by its former keeper. Even the story of its discovery cannot be verified one way or the other. Where this skull is concerned, it is particularly difficult to separate fact from fiction. That adds to its mystery—and to its allure.

The Mitchell-Hedges skull, fashioned out of clear Quartz, is about eight inches long, five inches wide, and five inches high. Weighing around twelve pounds, it is a humanoid skull with ridges, cheekbones, nose sockets, a detached jawbone, and deep eyeholes. Right up to the date of her death in 2007, Anna Mitchell-Hedges insisted that she had found "her skull" in the ruins of the Mayan city of Lubaantun on her seventeenth birthday in 1924. Anna was, she insisted, at the dig with her adopted father, author F. A. Mitchell-Hedges. She found the skull concealed in a ruined altar inside a pyramid. Her account reads like the script for an Indiana Jones movie (which is hardly surprising as some have suggested that the writer of *Indiana Jones and the Kingdom of the Crystal Skull* based the movie on this story). Anna claimed that she was lowered into a cavern teeming with large snakes and saw "something gleaming." When she picked it up, it was the skull. However, the facts that Anna appears in none of the photographs taken at the time and is not mentioned in official reports have been presumed to be evidence that she wasn't actually present at the dig.

Dr. Thomas Gann had been instructed by the governor of British Honduras (Belize) to survey the site of Lubaantun. Mitchell-Hedges joined that expedition in 1924. Gann makes no mention of the discovery of a skull in his survey report. Nor do the concurrent accounts of Mitchell-Hedges' fellow travelers Lady Richmond-Brown and Captain Joyce. A roistering adventurer and large-than-life character, Mitchell-Hedges is said to be the inspiration for the Indiana Jones character. From all accounts, including his own autobiography, he was something of a wild card. Opinions vary considerably as to how, and when, he obtained the skull.

Nevertheless, by the time Alice Bryant and Phyllis Galde wrote *The Message of the Crystal Skull* in 1989, the story of the finding had grown to almost mythic proportions. According to the book, the local Mayan people "danced and erected an altar on which to place it . . . The skull was worshipped as an ancient relic." The feasting continued for three days. Skull researcher Nick Nocerino told an even more embroidered tale with Mayans coming from far and wide to see the skull.[3] As a bribe to persuade the workforce to excavate once again, Mitchell-Hedges allegedly offered them the skull. Somehow, he retained ownership.

Similarly, tales of the skull's powers became legendary. Blue light was said to flash from the skull's eyes. It healed, but it also destroyed.

THE "SKULL OF DOOM"

Mitchell-Hedges and his daughter Anna were instrumental not only in creating mythos around the discovery but also the mystique regarding the skull's alleged baleful powers. Mitchell-Hedges was, after all, the author of several rollicking adventure novels. The idea of the "Skull of Doom" was taken up with enthusiasm by the metaphysical media.

In March 1962, an article in *Fate* magazine by John Sinclair appeared under the title "Crystal Skull of Doom." In it, Sinclair reported that when Mitchell-Hedges took the skull to Africa in 1949, a Zulu witch doctor apparently spat at the skull and performed a mocking dance in front of it. He was allegedly killed by a flash of lightning out of a clear blue sky. A similar tale told of a news photographer around the same time who yelled, "Will me to death. Rot!" as he was photographing the skull. One version says he was hit by a truck as he left, another that his darkroom blew up. According to the same article, Mitchell-Hedges begged Anna to bury the skull with him, saying: "Priceless as this treasure may be, it is a thing of evil and must die with me." All part of the mystique. In the 1950s, *Psychic* magazine similarly reported that three women had died after viewing the skull.

According to Mark Chorvinsky and Douglas Chapman, who extensively researched these sources, the story of the mockery dance by the Zulu chief was lifted from a letter written by Clifford M. Hulley to Mitchell-Hedges suggesting that a witch doctor might want to steal the skull for its reputed powers.[4] Out of such small details the fertile mind of an author conjures many a terrible tale.

In a televised interview with Anna Mitchell-Hedges, Mark Chorvinsky asked whether the skull's cursing power hadn't been highly exaggerated. Anna Mitchell-Hedges replied: "You didn't know father did you? He was quite a kidder. He told those things to a reporter that he was having some fun with."[5] As a result, according to Chorvinsky, "So much for the Skull of Doom, its sinister curse debunked by none other than Anna Mitchell-Hedges." That takes no account of a sentence in Mitchell-Hedges' autobiography that would be deleted from later editions: "Several people who have cynically laughed at it have died, others have been stricken and become seriously ill." (see "The Case for the Defense?" below). This is how Chorvinsky sums up the situation after studying the skull for many years:

I find it ironic that . . . I have answers for almost none of the important questions about the Mitchell-Hedges crystal skull. While there are stock answers for many of the questions, they are just that. While there are speculations aplenty, they remain speculations. For starters, I cannot honestly say that we know with any degree of certainty who made the skull, how it was made, when it was made, and what purpose it served. These questions remain perplexing. The ambiguities surrounding the skull's origins and mystique have added to its legend and left ample room for its many interpreters to fill in the blanks with whatever they find meaningful.[6]

I know exactly how he feels! Perhaps not surprisingly, after Anna's death, the skull was renamed the Skull of Love by its present keeper, Bill Homann, Anna's devoted companion before her death.

THE CASE FOR THE PROSECUTION
The case against the Mitchell-Hedges skull being authentically ancient and/or originating from Lubaantun has two strands. The technical evidence as to its manufacture, which we'll review shortly, and a trail of ownership that purportedly leads back to a nineteenth-century antiquarian and purveyor of fake artifacts, Eugene Boban. That trail, however, has a crucial missing link.

THE FAKER AND THE ART DEALER
Boban was the official archaeologist to the Mexican court of Maximillian I and a member of the French Scientific Commission in Mexico. He sold skulls that later came into the possession of the British Museum, including the skull that entranced me, and the Musée du Quai Branly in France.[7] Although Boban purveyed many genuine artifacts, he also sold a quantity of "authenticated" fakes to museums around the world, including the Smithsonian.

In 1886 Boban moved his business to New York. An auction of several thousand artifacts included a crystal skull that was sold to Tiffany's, who sold it on to the British Museum. In all, Boban disposed of at least five crystal skulls to museums around the world. Dr. Jane MacLaren Walsh, anthropologist emerita at the Smithsonian Institute, tracked Boban's activities and scientifically examined various skulls supplied by him (see below), concluding that they were comparatively modern carvings.[8] No record exists of where Boban obtained his skulls.

Initially, the Mitchell-Hedges skull was known as the Burney skull. In 1933, Sidney Burney, a London art and antiquities dealer, had acquired a skull of nearly identical proportions to the Boban specimen acquired by Tiffany's and sold to the British Museum. There is no information about where he obtained it, so it is merely supposition, but one frequently made by skeptics, that it was originally also supplied by Boban. When attempting to sell it to the American Museum of Natural History, Burney stated it was from Mexico. A close replica of the British Museum skull, it is almost exactly the same size and shape, although with more detailed modeling of the eyes and the teeth and a separate mandible. The journal *Man* featured two articles on the skull in 1936. The first entitled "A Morphological Comparison of two crystal skulls," and the second a comment on the first article by Adrian Digby. Digby reported that he could not find a provenance for the Burney skull prior to January 1934. In 1943, it was sold at Sotheby's in London to F. A. Mitchell-Hedges.

Burney was an old school friend of Mitchell-Hedges. Skeptics argue that the Sotheby's sales receipt proves that Anna Mitchell-Hedges could not possibly have found the skull years earlier on her seventeenth birthday. Believers argue that Burney could possibly have been keeping the skull on behalf of Mitchell-Hedges. By acquiring the skull at auction, Mitchell-Hedges became the legal owner, thus avoiding having to confess that he had illegally removed it from the Lubaantun excavation (see below). Anna Mitchell-Hedges herself explained that the skull was in Burney's possession as collateral for a loan. To her father's chagrin, Burney's son put the skull up for auction. Mitchell-Hedges frantically dashed to the auction to reacquire what had been his property. Years later in an interview, Anna said the loan had been paid off just in time, and the skull withdrawn from sale. But the Sotheby's receipt still exists. The true facts will probably never be known.

THE SCIENTIFIC EVIDENCE

If the Mitchell-Hedges skull did genuinely originate from Lubaantun, then it could be Mayan. The site was abandoned around 800 CE, so the skull would have to have been made before that date with pre-Columbian lapidary technology. The skull would have been fashioned with sharpened stone or possibly copper tools, and polished with sand. It would exhibit appropriate random markings with a slight twist, indicating the movement of the hand wielding the tool. By contrast, modern diamond-coated, high-speed rotary cutting tools leave lines that are perfectly straight.

It is claimed that the Mitchell-Hedges skull was examined at Hewlett-Packard in the 1970s when it had been lent to Frank Dorland, a crystal carver and skull researcher. As so often happens with these skulls, it would appear that there is no extant record of the examination at Hewlett-Packard, despite the fact that photographs were seemingly taken at the time. They certainly examined other skulls.[9] Dorland stated that the skull was carved against its natural axis, which would be a difficult task as the crystal could easily shatter. He reported that Hewlett-Packard found no microscopic scratches from metal tools. Dorland conjectured that the skull had been roughly hewn with diamonds and finished by polishing with silicon sand. He calculated that it would have taken up to three hundred years to complete.

Technology has moved on since 1970. According to Professor Jane Walsh, after Anna Mitchell-Hedges' death in 2007, her skull was taken by her former companion to the Smithsonian for testing. Walsh, who had already extensively tested the British Museum skull, said: "It seemed to me to be a close copy of that object, at least in size and shape. However, it differed from the British Museum example in its more elaborate carving, extremely high polish, and separate mandible."[10] A superimposed outline of the two skulls showed how close they were in shape. The initial study included examining the skull under a high-powered microscope and with a CT (computerized tomography) scan.

Walsh took two sets of silicone molds for scanning electron miscroscope (SEM) analysis of the tool marks. The molds revealed the marks of high-speed carving tools on the skull's surface. Deeply cut parallel ridges had been left by permanently embedded diamond residue. Impressions of wheeled tools were visible in the carved elements of one of the teeth. Under higher magnification, the polished areas exhibited parallel lines with a skipping pattern, indicating the use of a high-speed tool. Not something normally available in 800 CE. Walsh concludes:

> It seems reasonable to conclude from the SEM images that the Mitchell-Hedges skull was carved in modern times with high-speed, diamond-coated rotary burring and cutting tools of minute dimension. The teeth alone show the use of a rotary cutting tool less than 2 millimeters in diameter. I believe that the technology under discussion is decidedly 20th century. Considering the skull's initial appearance in the 1930s, I believe it was created at about that time. The British Museum skull, from which I believe this is copied, was on exhibit fairly continuously from 1898.

It appears, therefore, that the tale of the discovery may be a fabrication by Anna Mitchell-Hedges. Despite Walsh's dating it to the 1930s, it has also been suggested that it is possible that Mitchell-Hedges, a noted practical joker, purchased the skull in the 1920s knowing it to be a fake. He then hid it in the ruins for his adopted daughter to find as a birthday present. There are, of course, those who still assert that an ancient, much more techno-logically advanced civilization, or one from the stars, could have created it eons ago and deposited it with the lost civilization of Atlantis and from there it passed to the Maya and ultimately to Anna Mitchell-Hedges.

THE CASE FOR THE DEFENSE?

Before his death, Philip Coppens, a Belgian researcher into fringe science and speculative history, suggested a rather differ-ent reason as to why Mitchell-Hedges might have deliberately hidden the true origin of the skull.[11] At a Megalithomania con-ference in Glastonbury in 2008, Coppens discussed the skull and the then-forthcoming movie *Indiana Jones and the Kingdom of the Crystal Skull.* I was present for the discussion, and Coppens was very persuasive as to the skull's authenticity. The online YouTube video of that talk shows images of several skulls and of Anna Mitchell-Hedges, together with a survey of the "evidence" and an account of Mitchell-Hedges' life that may assist you in making up your own mind.[12]

In the first UK edition of his 1954 autobiography, *Danger My Ally,* written thirty years after the event, Mitchell-Hedges included brief information about the skull, but refused to say how he acquired it. The little information given was deleted in later editions and never appeared in the US version. In a chapter entitled "The Skull of Doom and a Bomb," there is a full-page picture of the skull. Mitchell-Hedges writes:

We took with us [to Africa in 1948] also the sinister Skull of Doom of which much has been written. How it came into my possession I have reason for not revealing. The Skull of Doom is made of pure rock crystal and according to scientists it must have taken 150 years, generation after generation working all days of their lives, patiently rubbing down with sand an immense block of rock crystal until the perfect Skull emerged. It is at least 3,600 years old and according to legend was used by the High Priest of the Maya when performing esoteric rites. It is said that when he willed death with the help of the skull, death invariably followed. It has been described as the embodiment of all evil. I do not wish to try and explain this phenomena.[13]

According to Coppens, there may have been a good reason for the omission. Had such a skull been found, title should automatically have passed to the expedition's financiers rather than to Anna Mitchell-Hedges and her father. As Mitchell-Hedges steadfastly refused to divulge its source, his publishers prudently removed a potential bone of contention from future editions. Mitchell-Hedges then legally acquired the skull at auction in 1943.

Coppens also quoted a 1999 interview with Patsy Wilcox, the owner of a guesthouse in Polperro, Cornwall. She stated that in the early 1930s Anna and her father stayed at the guesthouse with "a most unusual crystal skull, which they kept in a cupboard in one of the rooms they rented." However, the source for the quote is not referenced and cannot be followed up.

So, the Mitchell-Hedges mystery remains. It will no doubt go on generating explanations and theories for many years to come. Notwithstanding, there are a handful of skulls that have apparently been assigned to the ancient category after expert examination.

Amar: A Hand-Carved Skull

This anecdotal report is by the keepers of the Tibetan skull "Amar." Amar was reportedly brought over the Himalayas from its former home and is deemed by its keepers to be ancient (see page 6):

One of the world's foremost artists in the medium of quartz crystal sculpture carefully examined the crystal skull known as Amar in 2008. He determined that this crystal skull was definitely handcarved, and shows none of the tell-tale signs of machine carving or polishing tools or jewellers' wheel marks. Based on the markings on the crystal skull, he said that it would have been carved using a "bow drill," and would have taken many years to carve, perhaps even generations. He said that he had seen similar markings on Asian gemstone carvings dating from 650 AD (and potentially cylinder seals from 250 AD), and that this crystal skull could be that old. He was convinced that the features of this crystal skull appear to be a "portrait skull" probably based on the actual features of a very important person.

His parting words were: "I have not seen an ancient indigenous carving of this quality outside of a museum—in fact, this crystal skull really belongs in a museum."

It should be noted that while he is an expert in gemstone carving, he was very clear in stating that his beliefs are strongly rooted in skepticism with regard to all things pertaining to the esoteric or metaphysical properties of gemstones or crystal skulls. Therefore his findings about the Tibetan Crystal Skull are purely based on his extensive study and expertise of ancient and modern gemstone carvings, with no regard for any crystal skull lore or legends.

When I asked for further clarification on the expert consulted, this is what the skull's keepers had to say:

The artist made it clear that he is very much a skeptic himself—in fact, he told us that his favorite magazine is *Skeptic* magazine, and proudly pointed to a stack of them! Given this, we were amazed that he made the statements that he did about Amar—he was looking at it purely as a carving without being at all influenced by the "legends" or lore of crystal skulls. This actually made his conclusions even more valuable as he was completely objective. He made it very clear that he does not believe in the metaphysical aspects of crystals at all, and therefore we don't want to use his name. You can decide whether or not to use his comments without his name attached. He is a world-renowned carver of gemstones and quartz, and his work has been exhibited in prestigious galleries and art shows around the world, with dozens of articles published about him in magazines ranging from the *Lapidary Journal* to the *Robb Report*. He is definitely considered an expert in his field in the art of crystal carving, but he does not want to be associated with metaphysics in any way.

So, the report is presented here as it stands without attribution to source. It must be remembered that it was carried out without the latest scanning technology that could reveal subtle traces of machine-tool marks, or none if it is truly ancient. Once again, the question has to be asked, "Does it matter?" If it is a consciousness occupying the skull, or even its crystal matrix that is communicating, the answer surely has to be "not really." Amar communicated a message especially for this book (see pages 71–72).

Evidence from Other Skulls

In April of 1996, the BBC, in association with the British Museum, produced a documentary showing tests to determine the age of various skulls through use of an electron microscope. It included their skull and that of the Smithsonian. They also tested a skull from Guatemala, an ancient gold- and silver-plated reliquary cross that rested in a small carved crystal skull, and a further small skull. Anna Mitchell-Hedges was invited to attend with the Mitchell-Hedges skull. However, she declined.

A team including Margaret Sax, from the British Museum in London, together with Professor Ian Freestone, from Cardiff University, used sophisticated techniques to examine the skulls. It was determined that the British Museum skull had been carved using methods from the 1800s, most probably from Brazilian crystal. The museum's website states:

> The solid inclusions near the base of the skull consist of small green crystals . . . Using Raman spectroscopy, the green inclusions were shown to be an iron-rich chlorite. These minerals are found in mesothermal metamorphic greenstone environments. Sources of this type are not found in Mexico or within the ancient Mexican trade network . . .
>
> According to Museum records, the skull was acquired in 1897 from Tiffany and Co., New York, through Mr. George Frederick Kunz. In one of his numerous publications, Kunz claims that the skull was brought from Mexico by a Spanish officer before the French occupation. It was sold to an English collector and acquired at his death by Eugène Boban, a French antiquities dealer, later becoming the property of Tiffany and Co.[14]

An article, printed in the *Journal of Archaeological Science*, postulated that these skulls were actually made in Germany. However, reports differ as to whether the Smithsonian's skull had been carved in the 1800s or the mid-twentieth century. The skull held by the Smithsonian had been donated to the museum anonymously in 1992, along with a note saying it had been bought in Mexico in 1960. The British Museum skull had been worked with a harsh abrasive such as corundum or diamond. X-ray diffraction analysis showed that a different material, Carborundum, was used on the Smithsonian skull. Carborundum is a synthetic abrasive that only came into use in the twentieth century. "The suggestion is that it was made in the 1950s or later," said Professor Freestone. Professor Freestone said the work did not prove all skulls were phony, although it did cast doubt on the authenticity of other examples: "None of them have a good archaeological provenance and most appeared suspiciously in the last decades of the twentieth century. So we have to be sceptical," he explained.[15]

Various other "ancient" skulls have allegedly been tested. Sha Na Ra (see page 56) and Max (see page 59) were apparently shown to be carved by methods used more than five thousand years ago. Yet again, it has been impossible to consult the source report.

The Psychic Approach

The Pelton Foundation of Applied Paranormal Research, the Institute of Psychic and Hypnotic Sciences (Nick Nocerino's foundation), and the Society of Crystal Skulls, International, tried a different approach to the skulls. They brought in experts in the field of psychometry, scrying, and crystal gazing in an attempt to learn more. Pelton reports that "this provided glimpses of the past and wonderful scenarios of ancient ceremonies. A connection with the fabled Atlantis was also brought out during one of the sessions." As with Nocerino, Pelton found that specific colored light repeatedly took him into the same time frame. The Rainbow, Sha Na Ra, ET, Jesuit, Max, Agate Chip, and other skulls were also subjected to x-rays, laser light penetration, and macro-filming of the interior.[16] They cooperated with the BBC in bringing more advanced technology to bear (see above). I was unable to access the original reports.

Skullduggery in San Luis Valley

Just how easily a crystal skull saga may be misinterpreted—and how the story proliferates—is shown by a tale extracted from *The Mysterious Valley* by C. O'Brien on *www.ourstrangeplanet.com.*[17] The writer, presumably C. O'Brien, although this is not explicitly stated, relates how he received a phone call from Tom Blunt, an ex–Air Force intelligence officer, suggesting that he examine an artifact that had been dug up on a neighboring ranch. The owner had been touring her new property when her young companion noticed a glint of light from the ground. Stopping to investigate, they found a highly stylized but misshapen alien skull.

When the writer went out to examine it, it didn't appear to have been carved, but rather poured from molten glass. Stating that it was bound to stimulate controversy, the writer says, "However, regardless of its origin, there is no question that the find is an exceptional work of art." The rancher reported that some people were extremely scared when they saw it, and weird events began as soon as they discovered it. A spare tire on a truck exploded, her son and husband were injured when they took it off the property. The video camera with which the writer was documenting it inexplicably stopped working. A psychic reading said: "It is very old. It's not man-made and not of this Earth. You must be very careful with it. It can be very detrimental . . . You must be balanced, or you will be hurt." When the rancher asked the psychic if she should do anything in particular with it, he told her, "You don't need to do anything. Someone you didn't contact about it will appear and help do what needed [sic] to be done." The writer offered to have it authenticated, but speculated at the time that it could be an important artifact or an ingenious hoax. The story flew like wildfire through the crystal skull community, articles were written, and a channeler received a number of messages from it.

By the time C. O'Brien's book *Enter the Valley* was written a year or so later, the writer had an answer.[18] The skull had been created by Brad Chadez, a glassblower at the Blake Street Glass Company in Denver. Chadez made Day of the Dead skulls to sell in New Mexico. His family owned the ranch next door. He had buried the skull, a glass "second," as a talisman. As the writer says:

> As with most true "mysteries" there are usually no easy answers. The innocent little "ant-person skull" has had quite an effect on people. The reported strange phenomena that seemed to surround the skull still have no obvious explanations. Exploding tires, sickened babies, bashed in heads, broken video cameras and various other "unexplained" phenomena have been associated with the skull and may give us some insight into the true nature of "perceived" power-objects. Perhaps if enough people think something is magical, and focus their intent on it, then maybe a mundane object can actually become magical. The discovery of the skull, and the subsequent wide-flung notoriety it has received, may be a lesson for all who have a real need to believe in a so-called "mysterious" power object.

Untapped Sources

An Internet trawl to examine images of skulls threw up a blog that immediately caught my attention because of the intriguing photographs. If these images are genuine, and there is no reason to believe they are not, they show some crudely carved skulls that could well be ancient Mesoamerican together with other more detailed skulls that could just as easily be genuine or an elaborate fake.

Eric Vasallo, an anthropologist and archaeology graduate of the University of Miami, was in Mexico City in 2013 to seek skull evidence from ancient sites with the Oracle Stone Productions tour group. The Oracle Stone group had previously organized a crystal skull conference on 12.12.12 hosted by a Mayan shaman, which Vasallo had attended. He was acquainted with several "ancient" skulls. He described sitting with them as rather like being plugged into an electrical circuit or using a Bluetooth app.

In Mexico City, the group was invited to the home of muralist Diego Rosales, who had for decades investigated "the possibility that the Aztecs were seeded and/or inspired by Atlantean refugees and that they probably used these skulls that have been found in ancient sites all over the world much as we use smart phones, to connect them to other worlds and/or dimensions."[19]

Rosales showed them his collection of artifacts, including numerous skulls and objects gifted to him by local people. One, crudely carved in a green stone, had been given to him by a road worker in Tula, who had uncovered it from beneath a ceramic slab. Others had, apparently, been looted from beneath a mountaintop temple near Taxco, the burial of "an important ancient shaman or leader." Vasallo approached the archaeological authorities in Mexico regarding these skulls, but was told there is little money for excavation, conservation, or acquisition of artifacts. The museum in Mexico City has only one small crystal skull in its entire collection. It may be that at some time in the future, examination of Rosales' collection will add to our knowledge of skulls, although there is no documented evidence or provenance as to the dates of discovery or the locations from which they came. In the meantime, it is impossible to tell how genuine they are.

Then comes a story that could be an elaborate hoax on unsuspecting tourists . . . or not. No money changed hands. A young couple showed the leader of Vasallo's tour group a large skull which, they said, was causing strange things to occur, and the young wife to despair as it haunted her dreams. From the photograph, the skull looks remarkably like the Mitchell-Hedges skull. It could potentially be a carving from the same era. The skull had reportedly been looted from a "jungle location in Mexico." A medium, Jane Doherty, who was traveling with the tour group, was called in. She stated that the skull was one of a pair. The young man confirmed it was so. The other was in the possession of a friend. Jane Doherty recommended that the pair be reunited, as they were a male and female who belonged together, which was why one was causing trouble. (It should be noted that the couple did not try to sell the skull, so this was not an attempt to scam the group out of money.)

In order to find out the truth about the skulls, Eric Vasallo suggests:

> We must sift through all the information from all sources available. Talk to tourist guides, locals, archaeologists, grave robbers, psychics, shaman, specialists or engineers in related trades, ancient scripts from old archives, libraries or museums; synthesize all the information, simmer it down to a reduction and apply a finely tuned bullshit filter, in order to get to some semblance of what the truth is. It is a lot of work but the rewards are life and history changing . . . If we all cooperate together we may just be able to find the true, corrected "story of us," possibly within this generation.

Excellent advice, and exactly what another archaeologist has proposed. According to Michael E. Smith, who is a professor in the School of Human Evolution & Social Change at Arizona State University and is affiliated with the Colegio Mexiquense in Toluca, Mexico, the problem is lack of publication and lack of documentation of finds:

None of the likely authentic ones [skulls] have been published (see Smith 2004 on problems caused by the lack of publication of museum collections). The example I consider the best candidate as an authentic crystal skull was found at an Aztec site while I was there as an undergraduate. I remember thinking that Mesoamerican archaeology was quite cool indeed if things like crystal skulls came out of every site. Unfortunately that was the last crystal skull I have seen with a reasonable archaeological context.[20]

In a letter to NPR following a broadcast on the skulls, he pointed out:

The museum curators you interviewed proved that several phony-looking crystal skulls the size of footballs are indeed fakes. But they have not shown that the more abundant small crystal skulls are also forgeries. My colleagues and I have excavated many small ritual objects and jewelry of rock crystal at Aztec sites. Although none of the small crystal skulls now in museums come from documented excavations, I consider it extremely likely that they were indeed made by the Aztecs.

He gives his reasoning:

✳ The Aztecs produced many small objects out of rock crystal, mainly jewelry and ritual items. I have excavated a number of these at every site I've worked at. Some of the nicer crystal objects from Mexican museums are illustrated in Serra and Solis (Serra Puche and Solís Olguín 1994).

✳ Skulls were a major iconographic element in Aztec religious art. They are found in the codices, painted and modeled on pottery vessels, carved in stone sculptures and reliefs, etc. Although associated with the death god, skulls were not ominous objects of doom and gloom as in western culture; rather they were symbols of life, fertility, and regeneration (Baquedano 1998).

* There are a number of small crystal skulls in museum collections, just as there are numerous objects of clearly authentic Aztec date. Although it is difficult to generalize, my experience with museum storage collections suggests to me that many or most of these objects are legitimately pre-Columbian and not forgeries.

* There are other Aztec ritual objects in museum collections that we can be virtually certain are legitimate pre-Columbian items, yet none have been recovered from documented archaeological excavations. Obsidian mirrors are probably the best example.

In a comment on the blog, Devon Ellington said: "Great piece. And it reemphasizes the need to look at each artifact individually, not make blanket assumptions."

At this point I leave you to ponder the evidence and make up your own mind.

CHAPTER 3

Stone Heads
from Around the World

Carved stone heads are found in Easter Island, Costa Rica, Indonesia, Italy, Egypt, South Africa, Ireland, Bolivia, New Guinea, India, and China. The tradition is worldwide. Long before the civilizations of South and Central America flourished, head cults were found throughout the ancient world. While not necessarily carved out of what would today be regarded as "crystal," heads were often cut from stone, which has a crystalline structure. However, some of the earliest heads are created from clay or are actual bone craniums filled with clay, plastered, and painted to resemble heads. "Ancestral heads" such as these were venerated and reputed to be sources of great wisdom. From these archaic roots the crystal skulls emerged.

Neolithic Burial Rites

At Tell Qaramel in northern Syria, which dates to between 11,000 and 9650 BCE, human skulls were buried in small groups. The skulls were plastered with clay to recreate the face and then painted with skin-like color. Archaeologists interpret this as indicating a belief in the continuing influence and spiritual presence of deceased members of the tribe. In other words, a belief that consciousness continues after death and offers guidance. Similarly decorated skulls have been found in ancient Jericho (dated circa 12,800–10,500 BCE), the Nazareth Hills of Lower Galilee, and close to Petra in Jordan. The skulls have a distinctive overbite and cowrie shells inserted to represent eyes or painted black lines to indicate closed eyes. Skulls from Tell Aswad, a Neolithic settlement in southern Syria, exhibit the same characteristics. It seems clear that the whole of the Eastern Mediterranean had a long-standing skull culture. These skulls could well be the ancestors of later stone portrait heads.

Early Portraiture

Some of the earliest stone-carved heads discovered so far come from Göbekli Tepe in southeastern Turkey. Dating to the earliest Neolithic period, around 12000–10000 BCE, Göbekli Tepe is currently regarded as the most ancient human-built place of worship. Excavation of the site has revealed several huge, detailed "portrait heads" that may well have been attached to large statues. Excavation has also uncovered a much more stylized head reminiscent of the modernist Cycladic sculptures from the Greek Aegean Islands, created much later, from 3300–2000 BCE. One of the skulls shows a striking resemblance to the rather abstract skulls photographed by Eric Vasallo in Mexico.[1] Similar stylized stone heads representing humans and animals have been found at Nevali Cor in Turkey, dated to 8400 BCE. The presence of decorated skulls inside the shrines at this site and settlements in Çayönü and Çatalhöyük suggests that there was a common ritual practice involving skulls and shamanism all around Turkey for several millennia.

Varna's Golden Men

In the 1970s, Bulgarian archaeologists stumbled upon a vast seven-thousand-year-old Copper Age necropolis near the modern-day city of Varna on the shores of the Black Sea. The oldest gold-based civilization yet found, it was an extremely advanced one. Exquisitely crafted gold and beautifully faceted crystal jewelry were part of the complex funerary rites, so were equally well-crafted clay masks and heads. The necropolis contains the first examples of high status male burials in the area. Formerly, only females had been so honored. In one case, a complete, very high status burial lacked only the body of the deceased. Archaeologists describe it as a "ritualistic cenotaph," or symbolic burial. A clay head was placed where the skull should be, surrounded by golden offerings of the highest quality. Ritualistic cenotaphs were common not only in Varna, but throughout the world in the Neolithic period. The incorporation of symbolic objects for use in the "otherworld" strongly suggests a belief in life after death. It is a small step from there to a belief in communication with the spirits of the ancestors and wise beings from other realms.

The Olmecs and the Gulf Culture

The complex and somewhat mysterious Olmec culture flourished around the Gulf of Mexico beginning somewhere between 5000 and 4000 BCE, ending around 400 BCE. It has been described as a "mother culture."[2] The Olmecs had writing, mathematics, and a sophisticated calendar system. Enormous stone heads were created from giant basalt boulders. Basalt, a volcanic rock, is strongly magnetic. In ancient Egypt, basalt was regarded as powerfully magical and used for statues that were to be a receptacle for the gods. Small masks were also created in Serpentine. The distinctive Olmec heads portray mature men with fleshy cheeks, flat noses, and slightly crossed eyes, believed to be powerful rulers. Olmec-style masks carved from Jade have also been recovered.

The Mixtec culture flourished a little later, and these excellent craftsmen also produced stone, clay, and metal masks and heads. A Mixtec tripod vase features a detailed skeleton and the theme of death occurs frequently, as it does in Toltec art. The Mixtec's skill in carving hard stone was extraordinary. They fashioned rock crystal, Jadeite, Amethyst, Opal, Obsidian, Jet, and Agate into people with elaborate dress.[3]

So far, it would seem, no explicitly crystal skulls have been discovered from those eras.

The Skull of the Smoking Mirror

In an article in the *Bulletin of the International Association of Paleodontology* entitled "Damien Hirst's Diamond Encrusted Skull & Jeweled Skulls in Archaeology," the writer describes a Jade encrusted skull from Oaxaca, Mexico. It was formerly kept at the convent in Iglesias Santo Domingo:

> The mask is believed to represent the god Tezcatlipoca, one of the Aztec creator gods. He was also the god of rulers, warriors and sorcerers. His name can be translated as "Smoking Mirror." Its base is a human skull. Alternate bands of turquoise and lignite mosaic work cover the front of the skull. The eyes are made of two discs of iron pyrites set in rings made of shell. The back of the skull has been cut away and lined with leather. The jaw is movable and hinged on the leather.[4]

Similar Aztec masks have been discovered elsewhere.

The Maya too developed a refined technique for making objects of Jade and stone. Lifelike Jade masks with Obsidian and shell eyes have been found, but no documented crystal skulls have been unearthed as yet.

The Central Andes and the Skull Cults

Beginning somewhere prior to 1800 BCE, in the Central Andes, the taking of heads for ritual use has a long history that moves through successive cultures including the Chavin, Cupisnique, Moche, Paracas, Nasca, Huari, Chimu, and Inca. The skulls were carefully prepared and preserved. The "trophy heads" were held in the hands or attached to the belts of shamans and warriors, although certain temples have "skull racks" to hold them.

In 1926, Alfred Kroeber found the body of a beheaded corpse in a cemetery in the Nasca Valley. A ceramic vessel in the shape of a head had been placed in the tomb as if to serve as a substitute.[5] Similar Nasca "head jars" have been found that clearly depict all the characteristics of a severed head, and others that may well be a portrait of the decapitated victim. In cultures that so prized trophy heads, skulls may well have become part of the shamanic rituals. They may also have been recreated in other materials as precursors to the crystal skulls.

China, Mongolia, and Tibet

In her book *Crystals Skulls & The Enigma of Time*,[6] Patricia Mercier speaks of working with Mongolian skulls procured by an American shaman named Lionfire, also known as David R. Leonard. Lionfire acquires ancient crystal skulls from Mongolia that date to 3500 BCE. According to Lionfire, new archaeological evidence is showing that matriarchal, seminomadic tribes roamed the Himalayas between China, Tibet, and Mongolia in Neolithic times, and that these tribes carved stones and crystals into skulls. He states that virtually every tomb excavated for the Liaohe River dam site in China contained carved skulls. Once again, no archaeological reports are cited. Apparently Jade, Obsidian, Agate, Turquoise, Quartz, and other crystal skulls carved in an extremely sophisticated manner were also found in Inner Mongolia and elsewhere.[7]

Other reports on Chinese skulls are intriguing, as they include crystal skulls that are allegedly ancient. As ever, it is impossible to follow up with any degree of certainty. Sources speak of twenty-two ancient skulls being excavated in remote mountains on the

Chinese and Tibet borders. These were reported anonymously and linked to an extraterrestrial civilization from a crashed spacecraft, so this has to wait for evidence to be produced that verifies the claims. There are, however, several ancient skulls in Chinese museums.

Tibet has a long-standing skull cult, going back to the Bon religion that preceded Buddhism. Bone skulls were used in the creation of ritual artifacts, such as cups.[8]

Curious as to whether there was also a crystal skull tradition in Tibet, I contacted two Englishmen who have extensive contacts with exiled Tibetan monks and asked them to inquire about the skulls for me. Michael Maclaire-Hillier, proprietor of Spiritual Sky (an Internet site selling artifacts from the Himalayas), told me that the monks reported that small, crudely carved skulls would be used for meditation or as a part of a necklace. The monks were adamant, however, that these were never large or carved from Quartz crystal, only from local stones or Jade. They were for personal rather than ritualistic use. A similar reply came from my other source. The exiled monks were simply not aware of a crystal skull tradition in Tibet.

Mythology and Artifacts Meet in the British Isles

In ancient Britain the Celtic hero Bran the Blessed was the keeper of ancestral memories. When wounded in Ireland, he gave orders that his head—the container for his powerful wisdom—be removed and interred in the sacred White Mount, now the Tower of London. However, his followers took their time about this. For seven years they stayed in Harlech, "entertained by the head which continued to speak and knew nothing but joy and mirth." It took another eighty "timeless" years before his wish was granted and he was interred in the White Mount to act as a protective talisman for the British Isles. Arthurian lore says the king had Bran's head dug up to assist in the fight against invaders. When consulted, Bran taught everything he had learned from the Goddess' Cauldron of Rebirth, passing on his wisdom to future generations. Archaeological evidence has shown that the head cult was popular amongst the Celts. Stone-carved heads have been discovered from across the Celtic World and, in Provence in France, a gruesome skull-covered altar has been unearthed. A beautifully detailed stone "triple head" was discovered close to the ancient sacred site of Knowlton Henge in Dorset. Roman records refer to the Celts as headhunters who kept the severed heads of their enemies as trophies. Once again, no crystal skulls have been found.

CHAPTER 4

Crystal Skull Mythology

We've already glimpsed a little of the vast *history* of stone heads, but a *mythology* has also grown up around the crystal skulls quite unlike any other. In some cases, the details may have been deliberately set up to mislead, as it would appear to be the case with the Mitchell-Hedges Skull of Doom (see page 16–24). In others, the stories are purportedly ancient, passed on orally by indigenous peoples. Even this is contested. The mythology has grown exponentially over the last thirty years or so as the skulls have increased in popularity. We can start with the Day of the Dead, a practice based on a mythology that is at least three thousand years old.

The Day of the Dead

Although modern society tends to associate skulls with death and, in some cases, with evil, this was not the case in earlier times. Mesoamericans today celebrate the Day of the Dead, a ritual believed to have been carried out for at least three and a half thousand years. This ritual suggests that a skull cult from Mayan and Aztec times could well underlie the crystal skulls. Prior to Christianization, the Festival of the Dead took place throughout the whole month of August. Festivities were presided over by the goddess Mictecacihuatl, known as Lady of the Dead. Her role was to watch over the bones of the dead and preside over rituals honoring the ancestors. Mictecacihuatl was represented with a defleshed body, that is to say showing her bones and especially her skull.

When Spain conquered the area in the 1500s and Catholicism was imposed on the population, existing festivities were incorporated into Dia de los Muertos, the Day of the Dead. It was relocated to All Hallows and All Souls at the end of October. This is a period when, it is still supposed, the veils between the worlds are thin and communication takes place. Today, in Mexico people put on *calacas*, wooden skull masks, and dance in honor of their deceased relatives. The wooden skulls are placed on altars dedicated to the dead. Sugar skulls are eaten by a relative or friend, and glass skulls may be purchased.[1]

The Legend of the 13 Skulls

The basic elements of the 13 crystal skulls legend is that at a pivotal time in humanities history, the 13 crystal skulls will be reunited to awaken a new era—transforming from an old paradigm into a new world.

—Edwin Courtney

The most oft quoted legend about the skulls is that of the 13 skulls. The folklore is said to have been handed down from generation to generation of indigenous people. These stories involve thirteen crystal skulls, although an even older mythology concerning the Seven Major Crystal Skulls of Atlantis is also referenced as we will see. The legend of the 13 skulls was documented by the late skull researcher Nick Nocerino as being received from the skulls themselves.[2]

Myths and legends contain collective racial memories and spiritual truths presented through story and symbol. In many of the stories, it is said to be the Atlanteans who fashioned the 13 skulls that are reemerging today. However, some sources take the creation of the skulls back in time to before Atlantis—and to an extraterrestrial creation:

> Long ago, a Human cranium was manufactured out of Crystal and brought here from the Arcturus and Pleiades star systems. This sacred cranium was brought into the land of Lemuria, at a time when the Earth was still a zero point planet on a non-magnetic plane. The cranium is a symbol of the knowledge it contains. So the plan was for this Crystal skull to serve as the container for the perfect Human consciousness.
>
> Eventually, there was a total of thirteen skulls in Lemuria. They were placed in a sacred Temple, called Hiva, on a holy mountain known as Buelat. Made primarily out of quartz Crystal, these skulls were programmed with a vibrational frequency that emanates out from their structures.
>
> A second placement of skulls was made in the Temple of Poseida in Atlantis. But some of these skulls were lost in the Great Flood and during the exodus of Poseida, which occurred along a land bridge that connected it to the Mayan civilization on the Yucatan Peninsula. During that cataclysm, the thirteen Lemurian skulls were placed in dimensional lock in Tibet, where a secret order of Monks has been maintaining them.[3]

Two of these Tibetan skulls are said to have reappeared as Max (see page 59) and Amar (see page 57).

The "Mothers and Fathers of Wisdom"

According to Edwin Courtney and many other sources, a Mesoamerican myth, said to be carried forward from the Maya and Aztec civilizations, tells of thirteen crystal skulls belonging to the

Goddess of Death. Known as "the mothers and fathers of wisdom," each was carved from a single piece of crystal and had a moveable jaw. Rather than symbolizing death in the way that a skull does in the modern world, they reflected the view that death was just a passing phase, a doorway to another dimension. Through death, the spirit would rejoin the ancestors and the body would return to fertilize Mother Earth. These skulls were kept at specific sacred places guarded by priests and carried not only wisdom but also the gifts of telepathy and healing.

According to one version of the legend, after the Great Flood had destroyed the civilization of Atlantis, the survivors wanted to preserve their knowledge, so they carved 13 skulls. Of these, nine differently colored crystals represented the various races of humanity. Four were water-clear and symbolized the beasts that walk, crawl, slide, and fly. They were sent out around the planet, each kept at a different sacred site, guarded by keeper-priests, to await the time when the human race would have evolved sufficiently morally and spiritually to use the information they contained wisely.

Patricio Dominguez, a Pueblo spiritual adviser, asserted that "the crystal skulls are complete depositories of knowledge and each skull contains a particular specialist area of information—like a living library." Likening them to a set of encyclopedias, he goes on to say that, in the future, people will be able to read the information once the skulls have been gathered together again in one place. However, he warned that "the knowledge that is going to come out from the skulls is quite unimaginable to our current minds . . . But whether we humans then use that knowledge for good or for our own destruction is down to our preparations." He suggests that the skulls have emerged to "avert the catastrophe that man will wreak on the planet."

The Atlantean Ark

Several Native American nations share the legend of the 13 skulls, although this, like so much skull material, is strongly contested. The late Harley SwiftDeer Reagan, a somewhat controversial figure who claimed to be a Cherokee medicine man, reported:

> The skulls were kept inside a pyramid in a formation of tremendous power known as the Ark. The Ark was comprised of the twelve skulls from each of the sacred planets kept in a circle, with the thirteenth skull, the largest, placed in the centre of the formation. This thirteenth skull represents the collective consciousness of all the worlds. It connects up the knowledge of all the sacred planets.[4]

The idea of the Atlantean ark was taken up with enthusiasm by crystal skull workers and forms an important part of modern skull lore and crystal working. It is now regarded as "fact." This account cannot be substantiated. It is included here as an illustration of the lore that is circulating. This particular version suggests that there are twelve inhabited planets within the cosmos, each with its own skulls, and a thirteenth that acts as a bridge between the different worlds. Across the world, from the Mesopotamians, to the ancient Greeks, and right up into medieval astronomy, it was believed that the Earth was surrounded by crystalline spheres that contained the luminaries, planets, and fixed stars, and encompassed the whole cosmos.[5]

The Seven Major Skulls of Atlantis

In the legend of the Seven Major Skulls of Atlantis, a conclave of skulls was created and used in Atlantis before its destruction. The skulls related to the various planes of being and to the chakras that connect to them. They were said to be an integral part of the culture of Atlantis. According to Edwin Courtney:

The **Obsidian skull** related to the physical world and to the root chakra at the base of the spine. Used only by women, it was placed in the temple of the Divine Mother where it created a portal to the underworld. The skull was destroyed when Atlantis sank beneath the waves.

The **Coralite skull** related to the astral plane and the sacral chakra just below the navel. This created a portal to the astral realm and regulated the entire chakra system. It was destroyed in the Great Destruction.

The **Citrine skull** was connected to the lower mental plane and the solar plexus centre. Used only by the men of Atlantis, it was also destroyed at the fall.

The **Jade skull** was the portal to the emotional plane, being connected to the heart centre. Serving as a link to the ancestors, this skull contained the imprint of the consciousness of the wise ones of Atlantis. It is said to have survived the Great Destruction.

The **Morganite skull** connected to the throat centre and the Karma Rupa plane (home to the form assumed by a soul as an astral entity after death according to its karma and desires). It is said to have changed its composition due to the current dense vibrational field of the Earth and is now Quartz. It survived the fall and may be the skull known as Sha Na Ra.

The **Amethyst skull** was the portal to the brow, or third eye, chakra and the Bhuddic or Unity plane (location of the Akashic Record, this plane is where thought disappears and there is only knowing). It is said that this skull was permanently located in the Eye Tower in Atlantis. This skull survived and may be Ami, the most expensive skull in the world today (see page 55).

The Clear Quartz skull related to the crown chakra and the Atmic or Enlightened plane (the home of the spiritual masters and a place of "serene emptiness" where the Self becomes the external reality and there is only oneness). This was the Master Skull, the holder of White Light, which bound the conclave together. It was exclusively used by the Crystal Skull Master. This skull is sometimes claimed to have survived as the Mitchell-Hedges skull. Or, it could be said that that particular skull consciousness took up residence in the Mitchell-Hedges skull eons later.[6]

CHAPTER 5

Crystal Skull Consciousness: Human, Alien, or What?

Accounts differ widely as to the source of the consciousness that communicates through the crystal skulls. There are as many theories as there are skulls, some mind-boggling, others less so. It has been suggested that the consciousness is alien, star travelers from

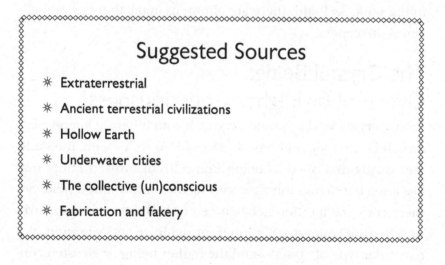

Suggested Sources

* Extraterrestrial
* Ancient terrestrial civilizations
* Hollow Earth
* Underwater cities
* The collective (un)conscious
* Fabrication and fakery

beyond this universe. Nick Nocerino, a prolific skull researcher, reported, "No matter how many skulls I have seen, I have to honestly say that wherever there are skulls, there is UFO activity."[1]

Other sources suggest that the consciousness is ancient but earthly: the sum total of collective human experience. Or that it comes from a race living within a hollow Earth. Or beneath the sea. From the ancestors. From the Source (All That Is).

Inner Consciousness?

Most skullkeepers agree that skulls have a higher, more evolved consciousness than that which presently exists on Earth today. Skeptical researchers such as Frank Dorland were more inclined toward an inner consciousness view in which, when looking at a skull, the keeper's own subconscious mind linked with the collective unconscious and communicated what it found there. The archetypal images so often interpreted as from "out there," may well be a part of the human psyche that is more usually accessed through dreams and such. Then again, the skull may be picking up the belief system of those who handle it, leaving behind a residual program to be read by the next person who connects to the skull. As I said, there are almost as many theories as skulls and skullkeepers.

The Crystal Being: Oversoul or Higher Consciousness?

From a crystal worker's view, a crystal has an inherent energy of its own. It is, after all, millions of years old. As we've seen, the skulls are usually described as being home to an evolved entity that has a separate consciousness with its own information field. So, there could be a difference between a skull's own crystal matrix or "oversoul" energy—the inherent qualities and vibration of a particular type of crystal—and the higher being or elevated consciousness that takes up residence in a skull.

Michael Eastwood runs the British crystal shop Aristia. He is the author of *The Crystal Oversoul Attunements*. Mike uses the description "oversouls" as a collective term for specific portions of crystalline consciousness. These oversouls are vast beings that inhabit another plane of existence but communicate with their crystals on Earth and with humans. In his view, each crystal of a particular type is linked to every other crystal of that type through the oversoul. So every Citrine, for instance, is connected to the Citrine crystal oversoul. Which means that all Citrines, no matter where they may be, communicate with one another through their oversoul, and they have the same properties. The oversoul acts as a kind of higher resonance or mentor for the Citrine family. It also gives assistance to a human being when requested.

The beings with higher consciousness, on the other hand, are perceived as not belonging to a specific crystal family, but rather to a vast, highly evolved consciousness with its own shared information field. Together these higher beings create the crystalline skull network. Facets of this consciousness take up residence in a skull in order to communicate and download energy. That is, the skull acts as a transceiver for a specific part of the consciousness and information field that expresses itself as an individual "personality." Which view you take is up to the individual skull-keeper. There is no reason why the two should not integrate and work together. However, the resonances need to be in harmony, or a skull will feel energetically wrong.

CHAPTER 6

Skullkeepers, Carvers, and Their Skulls

When the film *Indiana Jones and the Kingdom of the Crystal Skull*, which drew on existing skull mythology, was released in 2008, there was an explosion of interest in the crystal skulls. Skullkeepers had been working with their skulls long before that. We've already looked at the Mitchell-Hedges controversy and the nineteenth-century fakers. It's now time to examine contemporary skullkeepers and their skulls—and one or two pioneers who've passed on.

Skulls in America

AMI: THE MILLION-DOLLAR SKULL

It is rumored that one ancient Amethyst skull, Ami, which was on sale for over a million dollars, changed hands in 2009. The skull had been kept in a bank vault in San Jose, California, for many years, and, perhaps not surprisingly, remains there. It is a very dark purple Amethyst reputed to have sat on the desk of the former president of Mexico, Porfirio Díaz, who was president from 1876 to 1911. The president was of Mesoamerican Mixtec ancestry and had several skulls in his keeping. Ami reappeared in 1979 when a Mayan shaman priest, Francisco Reyes, purchased the skull, which was sent to the United States. In 1983 Ami was put up as collateral on a loan that was not repaid. It was acquired in 1985 by a group of businessmen. Research is reported to have been carried out by the laboratory at Hewlett-Packard, which had previously tested the Mitchell-Hedges skull. The laboratory is said to have concluded that no modern, high-pressure tools were used to carve the skull. Ami is, therefore, considered to be an ancient skull at least 1,500 years old. And, if the sale price rumors are true, of inestimable value. Like so much to do with the skulls, this report has so far been impossible to substantiate from primary sources.

NICK NOCERINO AND SHA NA RA

Sha Na Ra was discovered by the late Nick Nocerino in 1995 through "psychic archaeology." Asked to use psychometry to pinpoint an area where an artifact would be located, Nocerino says he indicated the spot where Sha Na Ra was later found in a terracotta basket. This large, clear Quartz skull was with another smaller but similar skull known as the Rainbow (because of the colors that dance within it). Other crystal artifacts were also found along with it. The site excavation is not publicly documented.[1] Nocerino was a professor of parapsychology who pioneered crystal skull research. In 1945 he became the founder and director of the Institute of Psychic and Hypnotic Sciences and began the Crystal Skulls Society, International in 1949. He was one of the original proponents of the 13 skulls legend, which was received through a skull he examined. Sha Na Ra was one of the skulls researched at the British Museum. Reputedly, no tool marks were found, although, once again, the primary source report cannot be accessed.

After her father's death, Michele Nocerino became the keeper of Sha Na Ra and offers private sittings and workshops with the skull. She says that her father became interested in the skulls after an encounter with one held by a secret society in France during World War II. During his lifetime Nocerino studied most of the extant ancient skulls from around the world. However, the only one he actually owned was Sha Na Ra. In an interview with Phil Jenkins, available online, Nocerino speaks of activating the codes contained within skulls by means of color, light, and sound. He describes seeing pictures through the "sutures" in the skull that could be transferred to other crystals. Nocerino regarded the skulls as "a doorway to a greater understanding of ourselves and our place in the universe in all its dimensions."[2]

JOSHUA SHAPIRO

Joshua Shapiro is one of the most active of the modern skull-keepers. He has been exploring crystal skulls for over thirty-five years. His first skull encounter was with Ami, the Amethyst skull described above. He and his partner Katrina travel around the world as "the skull explorers," facilitating skull conferences and seeking new skulls. A prolific author, Joshua graphically recounts his adventures. He is the owner of a skull family that includes, among others: Rosalita, a life-size skull; the Smoky Quartz skulls Portal de Luz and Geronimo Golden Eagle-Eye; and Heavenly Mother (Pacha Mama), a Rose Quartz skull.[3]

AMAR

Amar, an "exiled" Tibetan Quartz skull, is currently cared for by *CrystalSkulls.com*, but is said to originate from the Himalayas. He resides in a sanctuary in North America, attuning and charging up skulls that go out around the world. A portion of the proceeds supports exiled Tibetans to maintain their culture. Amar embodies the qualities of unconditional love and compassion. Reputedly, in his homeland he was used for divination—Tibetan Quartz facilitates access to the Akashic Record—and healing not only of the people but also the land and communities in which they lived.

CANA IXIM

The people at *CrystalSkulls.com* are also the current keepers of a Blue Jade skull called Cana Ixim. The name means Lady of the Corn. As they state on the *CrystalSkulls.com* website, "Corn represents the harvest of abundance, prosperity and plenty. It symbolizes female fertility and male virility." Cana Ixim is unusual in that it has markings carved in relief on the top of the cranium. His keepers at *CrystalSkulls.com* report:

> An expert in Mayan glyphs and symbols examined the rare glyphs that are carved in relief on the top of the Blue Jade Skull called Cana Ixim. He said that these were foundation glyphs that appear on Mayan temples. We were also told that these glyphs represent the alignment with the Galactic Rift and the return of the Solar hero. It is believed that the circular indentation carved in the crown was a vessel for liquid (perhaps even blood) during sacred ceremonies.

The skull was formerly held in Guatemala by a gentleman who, they said, wanted Cana Ixim to go to a healer "with a heart of love with good hands." The story is that it was found inside a cave that connects to the source of the river Sachichaj in a mountain about one hundred miles from Peten, Guatemala (referred to as authentic Mayan land). The Sachichaj River possesses a beautiful characteristic turquoise color, similar to the Blue Jade of Cana Ixim. According to *CrystalSkulls.com*, a "reliable source" in Guatemala reported that:

> The person tell me that the history he listen from his father and he was hear from his antecessors was that a few days before the skull appears or was found, in Guatemala was a big volcano eruption and a lot of people die, and the skull (Cana Ixim) appears to help and it

won't let that never happen again. They use it to heal sick people, snake bites, help woman pregnant (the head was collocate [placed alongside] in the stomach of the future mother), in ceremony for planting (in Guatemala the indigenous celebrate ceremonies to bless their plantations for good harvest). The most shocking cases are an old lady that can't move her fingers because has it rigid and twisted. After the ceremony of healing [when] she put hands on the skull she can move her fingers easily. A man that suddenly disappears a big mass (possible tumor) in his stomach.

Cana Ixim now joins with Amar in attuning crystal skulls to be sent around the world. (See page 57.)

MAX AND JOANN PARKS

Max is claimed to be an authentically ancient skull that shows no tool marks and could be thousands of years old. Max was apparently discovered in Guatemala and was reputedly used by Mayan priests for healing, rituals, and prayers. The story goes that Lama Norbu Chen, a Tibetan Red Hat lama, studied in Guatemala, where he came into contact with Max. When Lama Norbu left Guatemala, he was given the skull. He took him to Houston, Texas, where he was used as a spiritual and healing tool. The young daughter of JoAnn and Carl Parks had bone cancer and met Lama Norbu. JoAnn worked for the Lama for many years. Just prior to his death, he handed her the skull. Not knowing what to do with it, she placed it in a closet. Eventually, in 1987, JoAnn saw a documentary featuring Nick Nocerino, who had apparently been searching for Max since 1949. Following contact with him, she became an internationally recognized Peace Elder, offering healing and consciousness-raising sessions with the skull. JoAnn channels messages from Max and also allows other communicators to pass on information from him (see page 58).

CAROLYN FORD AND EINSTEIN, THE SKULL OF CONSCIOUSNESS

Carolyn Ford is the founder of Firedancer Vibrational Essences and is based in Sedona, Arizona. She has been active in the healing field for many years. She has been the keeper of Einstein since 1990, but did not make him public until 10.10.10 in New York City in conjunction with the Edgar Cayce Association for Research and Enlightenment. She did, however, introduce him to the late Nick Nocerino.

In an interview she was asked how Einstein came to her. Her reply was that in a workshop she had meditated with a contemporary skull who told her, "You are a guardian." So she began to look for a skull of her own. She called friends who had a crystal shop, requesting a small skull. When they called her back, they said they'd found her skull but there was a problem. It was bigger than she'd requested. Her friend Jack Frasl, one of the owners, suggested she meet the skull.

So she boarded a plane and came face-to-face with Einstein, a thirty-three-pound skull. She says, "When I met this very large skull, I was overcome with the feeling that this was my baby, I remembered my old dear friend . . . From the moment I met my new skull I fell in love. This skull was a part of me, past, present and future." She bathed the skull with rose water and began dreaming flower essence formulas, each having rose as a basic ingredient. She planted a vast rose garden. The rose essence represented love, and she was told that everything she did would be infused with love.

Jack told her that, the morning after her request, a man had called into the shop looking to sell artifacts from the estate of an explorer. The pieces had been brought back from expeditions during the 1930s and 1940s. When Jack saw the skull, he knew it was the one she was seeking. When she introduced the skull to her mother and stepfather, her stepfather immediately said, "Einstein." The skull had received his name.

HUMBATZ MEN

*It was written in the deepness of stars that the sacred crystal
skulls would return on the right time to guide mankind
and make them learn from the cosmic laws.*

—Humbatz Men

Humbatz Men is a Mayan elder and shaman who now travels the
world with the crystal skulls. He states that he reincarnated near
Chichen Itza in his present life to be in charge of reactivating
that sacred site and welcoming the Great Spirit there. "I will do
this together with my sacred skull which was granted to me by the
Great Spirit from the Himalaya Mount there in the sacred lands
of Tibet." On the winter solstice in 2012, he conducted a skull
ritual that activated a flow of energy in the Mayan ceremonial
centers and began a new cycle. For Humbatz Men, December 21,
2012, was a time when:

> All the initiates of the world will begin their initiation
> within this new cycle of 5,125 years. This is the only
> way to enter the dimension of the cosmic time, char-
> acterized by the universal and unified way of think-
> ing. Only then our cosmic brothers and sisters from
> beyond the universe will consider us like beings that
> will have evolved at a cosmic level.

He warns that,

> If we continue walking on this fake pathway of the
> so-called "progress," in which our human values are
> being manipulated by vain interests and every ruler
> thinks he has found a mine of gold, then we will be
> causing the destruction of our Mother Earth and our
> self-destruction. We will get lost in that pathway of the

no return, with no beginning or end, and then our gods will cry for so long that their abundant tears will make us get drowned in the sea of desperation . . . and finally, the winds will blow so strongly that they will blow away our spirits in order to purify them within the memory of forgetfulness.[4]

Earlier Humbatz Men had led a pilgrimage across America, and there is an account by Kevin Garnnett of his work at sacred sites with two hundred participants and crystal skulls.[5] In his account, Garnnett describes the scene:

> Humbatz, along with 6 elders took their skulls and walked around the circle of participants, offering everyone to touch foreheads with the skulls they carried, and thus pass the energy and power of the skulls into the participant and to imprint the signature and energy of the individual into the sea of color and information of the skull . . . This ceremony had a subtle yet profound effect upon me. Although, it felt surreal, it was neither out of place or uncomfortable. Being with Humbatz, the other elders as well as all those who had traveled to participate was very calming and comfortable to me.[6]

British Skullkeepers

EDWIN COURTNEY

Edwin Courtney is perhaps the most well known of the British skullkeepers, and he's the man who introduced me to their mysteries. I can do no better than to let him tell his story in his own words, written specially for this book.

When I think back, my journey with the crystal skulls began when I was a little boy watching *Arthur C. Clark's Mysterious World* on TV. The opening credits featured a beautiful revolving quartz crystal skull full of shimmering rainbows and clear white lights, a skull which I now realise was the Mitchell-Hedges skull. It is practically the only thing I remember now of that show, that beautiful object revolving in the light.

Skullkeeper Edwin Courtney
(Courtesy of Sam Armstrong)

Much later on, almost twenty years ago now, I bought my first crystal skull, a palm-sized optical Rose Quartz skull, which I later gave to my brother. I paid a ridiculous amount of money for it at the time—it was bought in a shop long since closed in Glastonbury. Knowing nothing about the skulls, their mysteries and legends, I just knew the skull was meant to be mine. I knew intuitively how it had to be held (how the Priests of Atlantis held them back in the day) and that was that! The Skull sat on my shelf, silent and lifeless for years, until finally I passed it on. I have regretted that act many, many times since, but a giveaway is a giveaway—especially where family is concerned!

Later still, once again in Glastonbury, I was leading a spiritual retreat when, during a healing treatment I was giving, my guide reminded me of a life-sized crystal skull I had seen in a shop called Stone Age the day before, made from bottle-green Obsidian. My guide insisted that I needed to buy it, but the price of the skull was way out of my league. "Go and talk to the shopkeeper," my guide insisted, but, fearful of sounding like every other new age nutcase claiming my guide told me to do it, I decided not to bother, and so tuned the guide out and carried on with my healing. That night I dreamt that a goddess came to

What Exactly Are the Crystal Skulls?   63

me in the Chalice Well Gardens where we were staying, holding the Obsidian skull in her hands. "Her name is Kaora," the goddess said, and, as she lifted the skull to her head, it transformed itself into a mask that she placed over her face! Not one prone to prophetic dreams, I realised someone was trying to tell me something, and so went to see Lui Krieg, the owner of Stone Age. To my utter shock, Lui was very keen for me to have the skull. He let me hold the skull, encouraging me to take it out of the shop and into the light. Lui told me he could see the skull reacting to my energy. I left with it, without paying a penny. Lui trusted that I would pay off the skull when I could. It took me three years in total, and even then dear Lui reduced the price in order to help me do so!

My first six months with Kaora were awful. She would not speak to me or through me until I was appropriately purified. I went through emotional hell, which was amplified by the fact that after only two weeks of having the skull, long before I paid even a pound for her, I dropped her, in her box, down a concrete flight of steps! She survived—despite rolling out of the box—with just a few dinks and chips. I would discover later that this incident was an echo of when I had been guardian of the Skull's consciousness in ancient Egypt, and I had allowed its vessel to be destroyed by a Priest of Set. Finally, when I was clear, Kaora began to speak both to me and through me, revealing much of that which I now teach concerning the skulls, such as the nature of their consciousness and Atlantean connections.

Since then, I have collected more and more skulls, both human and extraterrestrial. It seems to be a common trait amongst skull guardians—the obsession becomes almost an addiction. My fascination with skulls led me to a point at which I owned in excess of thirty skulls. It has only been recently that I have sold much of my collection, paring down my skulls to just those few that I continue to work with.

There is no doubt in my mind that the skulls have changed my life. They have literally opened my eyes to the truth and understanding that was previously beyond my understanding and reach. They have prompted the recall of powerful personal past lives concerning Lemuria and Atlantis, helping me to see why the consciousness of the skulls was created and what purpose they serve mankind now. I have performed readings with them, given numerous trance communications and healings, working both on individuals and the earth. I have worked with groups of people, in conjunction with other skull guardians, and alone, consciously, unconsciously, in dreams, and passively (simply carrying the skulls hither and thither as they silently and invisibly "do their thing"). I have witnessed incredible things brought about by their power: their ability to make themselves invisible, to call to people telepathically, to awaken people's dormant psychical ability, purge people of emotional blockages, as well as working directly upon the energy system to heal the physical body. I continue to work with them to this day. I'm always waiting for them to give me the green light as to when they need to be somewhere, what they need and want to do, always certain that it is I who work for them and never the other way around. I have had to endure some indignities along the way, such as taking the skulls all the way from Yorkshire to Surrey, where they insisted that not only did they not want to be touched, but they also didn't want to be seen! You try giving a lecture on skulls during which the skulls stay hidden in their box all evening. That, I can assure you, was not a fun thing to do. But I trust them, and I know that they have a higher purpose and understanding that is at times simply beyond my ken.

I have also always been clear that it is the energy within the skulls that is important, and never really the vessels themselves. I have met ancient skulls, brand new skulls, giant skulls, and teeny weeny skulls big enough to slip into your jeans pocket, and never felt that one was necessarily more powerful than any other. I have never bought into the idea that the skull has to be ancient or huge to be powerful. I believe instead that the consciousness, the unique spiritual intelligence within the skulls, which can shift and move from one skull to another as easily as our own spirit moves from body to body, is the key. The consciousness expresses its wisdom and power through contemporary and ancient skulls alike, whether they be indeed huge or small. This wonder means that the skulls are accessible to all, as they always intended themselves to be, available so that all of mankind might draw upon their power and wisdom for their own betterment and the betterment of the world.

ALPHEDIA ARARA AND SHERLING

Alphedia Arara is a Scottish crystal skull channel, caretaker, and earth-healer. She was formerly a press officer and environmental researcher in the Scottish parliament. She runs the Elemental Beings website and has been working with the skulls since 2009 after she acquired her first at the London Mind Body Spirit festival at Olympia. Since then, her collection has grown and now includes a twenty-seven kilogram Preseli Bluestone crystal skull. She also works with dragon skulls and unicorn skulls for earth-healing. All the skulls Alphedia works with are modern. In 2010, she acquired Sherling, an eleven-kilogram Merlinite earth-healer skull who works with the Crystal Skull Conclave. As Alphedia explains:

> The Crystal Skull Conclave is a consciousness that resides within crystal skulls. This consciousness is willing to work with humanity again at this time in the Earth's evolution and many are now drawn to be the guardians of crystal skulls. Sherling is a Grand Master of the Crystal Skull Conclave—who is here now to assist us with the passage through the turbulent times on Planet Earth as we pass through the ascension process and dealing with man's disruptive and destructive influence on his environment.

Alphedia's mission with the skulls is to take them and other earth-healers to sites, often in remote Scottish locations, to clear the land of trauma, rebalance earth energy anomalies, and reopen stargate portals. She works intuitively with the skulls and is able to hear their requests about the work they wish to do and their purpose for being on Earth. Sherling and some of her other skulls have collected codes and performed skull activations at sacred sites such as the Callanish Stones on the Isle of Lewis, inside Mendelssohn's Cave on the Isle of Staffa, Lindisfarne Priory, Avebury Stone Circle, Stonehenge, the Machrie Moor stones on Isle of Arran, Loch Buie stone circle on the Isle of Mull, and the stone circles at Kilmartin, the largest complex in the UK.

Alphedia Arara has also taken groups to locations such as Mount Schiehallion on 12.21.12 to work with the skulls to reactivate a ley line that travels from there in the center of the Scottish Highlands to the great pyramid in Eygpt. In 2013, she ran a

Alphedia Arara and some of her skulls (*Courtesy of Alphedia Arara*)

What Exactly Are the Crystal Skulls?

retreat to clear the land trauma of the Viking raids on the sacred holy isle of Iona, off the west coast of Scotland, and in particular the massacre of the monks on the beach. She has also taken the skulls to Glastonbury Abbey, Old Winchester Hill, Old Sarum at Salisbury, as well as doing activations with the dragon skulls in York Minster to clear blocked energy in the ley lines running through the old capital of England. She lives thirty minutes from Rosslyn Chapel and works with the skulls at the sun disk and on the rose line that runs through the magical glen there.

(A message from Alphedia's skull Sherling is included in chapter 7, and her earth-healing method is on page 138.)

The Carvers

RAVEN: SKULL CARVER EXTRAORDINAIRE

According to *www.ravensroost.net*, the website for the skull carver Raven, people frequently ask who Raven actually is. The reply is given that the reclusive Raven has been a rock hound all his life and deliberately maintains an air of mystery to protect his privacy. Ravenia, the webmistress, was about to write a piece for this book when life circumstances intervened. So they kindly gave permission for the website information to be used instead:

> Raven is a man steeped in mystery and, like his namesake, is secretive about his personal life. He has decades of experience in the lapidary trade and Raven values his reputation of being honest and fair. He deals in quality, this is apparent when you view the gemstones and jewels in his inventory.

This is something I personally vouch for. I own a Raven dragon skull, as does healer Jeni Powell (see page 81). I have had the pleasure of receiving guidance from her dragon skull Sofia, carved by Raven, as well as my own Morganna. All Raven's skulls are intricately carved and contain incredibly wise beings. This is not surprising as:

> Having a self taught working knowledge of how to cut stone has helped Raven to know how to perfect his merchandise. The selection of the rough stones is the first step. To understand what a piece will yield in cutting and polishing enhances the quality of the end product . . . Raven has been carving for approximately 30 years now. This has enabled him to develop a detailed carving style unique to his talents. Raven's [humanoid] skulls exhibit the neck attachments, hollowed out cheek bones, well defined hollowed out jaws and nasal cavities not present in skulls carved anywhere else.

Pictures of master Chinese carver Shan Gimn Wang carving the massive skull "Pepe" under the guidance of Raven are at *www.ravensroost.net/creation.htm*. Over two hundred hours went into the carving process, which is documented from its beginning as a thirty-five-pound lump of raw Quartz to the finished skull, which weighed in at 16.5 pounds. Pepe now resides in a private collection, as do many other Raven skulls.

LEONDRO SOUZA

Leandro Souza is a Brazilian master carver whose skulls are now exclusive to the Temple of Alchemy. As a master carver of more than twenty-five years, he carved the world's largest skull, Akator. Leandro's skulls contain very powerful beings of Light. They are charged by Akator. "His intuition allows him to be a clear channel to the crystal matrix and the skull that is being born from his hands. He listens to how a piece of crystal wants to be carved, which results in skulls with special features. There will be rainbows at areas such as the third eye."[7]

CHAPTER 7

Messages from the Skulls

Crystal skulls from around the world have been communicating their messages for some years now. While the information is filtered through the mind of each individual channeler, and therefore through their own particular mind-set, the messages are remarkably congruent. They address familiar themes such as earth-healing, planetary change, and the need for humanity to evolve. The first two messages were given specifically for this book through the keepers at *CrystalSkulls.com*. The keepers prefer to remain anonymous as they believe that the skulls are the messengers, not them personally.

Message from Amar

Amar communicated the following message to explain how the skulls work.

Crystals—particularly quartz crystals—are receivers and transmitters of energy and information. All crystals have conscious energy, but when crystals are carved into crystal skulls, they become beings of consciousness. Crystal skulls record everything that they have witnessed and store the energetic imprints or "memories" of these experiences. Computer memory chips are essentially made of quartz, and like a computer, a crystal skull can transmit energy and information into other crystal skulls in a type of wireless download. Many old and ancient crystal skulls have been used in various types of ceremonies and rituals because of their ability to enhance and amplify the power of intention. Some have been used for healing and divination, which enriches their energy. As with all crystals, crystal skulls can be powerful tools and allies for healing and enlightenment on all levels. When an old or ancient crystal skull energizes other crystal skulls, it shares its energy with them, imprinting them with the vibration of all that it has experienced. The energizing process further activates and attunes a new crystal skull to higher frequencies. The difference with an energized crystal skull is that its power and consciousness are more awakened, which those who are sensitive to energy can strongly feel and attest to. The purpose and mission of all crystal skulls is to raise the energetic frequency and consciousness of everything around them. This supports the Earth and all of her inhabitants in the process of change, transformation, and ascension that this planet is now undergoing. The more energized and activated a crystal skull is, the more empowering it can be for One and All.

Message from Cana Ixim

Cana Ixim speaks about ancient civilizations:

There are those who believe that ancient people were more rudimentary, barbaric, and less advanced than modern man. However, there are also those who marvel at the astounding complexity of ancient structures such as pyramids that cannot be duplicated even with today's science. Ancient languages and symbols may be lost to present civilizations, but that does not make them meaningless. The truth is that ancient man understood the connection between all things in this world and in this Universe, and these energetic connections were the foundation for everything. The Ancients recognized that crystal skulls were vessels, conduits, and amplifiers for higher consciousness, and used crystal skulls to access and record wisdom of all kinds. A modern computer contains vast amounts of information—but only for those who know how to access that information! There are those who might look at a computer as an empty box—they may also see a crystal skull simply as a carved rock! Why carve a rock into a skull? Because crystals are alive with energy, and the skull is the vessel for consciousness itself.

Message from Max

Perhaps one of the best known skulls, Max, travels the world with his keeper offering messages to humanity (see page 59). Through his keeper JoAnn Parks, Max says:

What am I about? I am about many things, however, that depends on your personal levels of growth and understanding. I am about Truth and Integrity and Respect. The Truth and Integrity are how I am represented. The Respect is of the crystal skulls and the indigenous people who created me.

I am here as a teacher and a tool. I am a connector that goes back to self. When you look into my eyes, you are looking at a reflection of your own self, of who you are, and who you aspire to be.

I am about peace and harmony and bringing people together. I am here to help bridge the gap between Races, Cultures, and Religions.

I am about healing. However, remember there are many levels of healing. There is physical, mental, spiritual, and emotional healing. All of these levels must be treated in order to heal what is sick.

I am about self, the reunion with your self and tapping into the path of higher consciousness. Each time an individual comes into contact with me, some shift in their consciousness occurs. That shift is generally around their ability to feel more connected to the self. I am here to gently awaken the sleeping giant of Spirituality that lays buried deep within humankind. I accomplish this with my unique gift of touching each individual in my own way.

All of this I do with the aid of my keeper, JoAnn Parks. She is the translator for those who wish to hear and learn about me and the very means by which I travel the planet. With JoAnn's help, I am no longer an old Rock Head hanging around inside the closet. I am now a Rock Star, presenting my message of unity around the world.

Max's Peace Message to the World:

P	is for the past mistakes for killing Mother Earth.
E	is for our effort in the sharing of her rebirth.
A	is for all mankind, Red, Yellow, Black, or White.
C	is for the courage it will take to make it right.
E	is not for easy. We'll have to fight with all our might to make this world a better place. Our love can make it right.

Mankind will not awaken until we learn how to blend each other's truths for love and peace. It all begins within. That is how we're going to make it, that is how we're going to win. The wars that we hate so much really do begin within. Until we trust each other and we learn how to bend, these wars will keep on raging right to the very end.

Put this all together and it spells PEACE for you and me where all can come together in a world that will be free.[1]

Alphedia Arara and Sherling

Scottish psychic Alphedia (see page 66) channels Sherling, a Merlinite skull, and other skulls from the Crystal Skull Conclave. Sherling regularly communicates regarding planetary changes and assists with deep earth-healing. He explains the role of the skulls:

The Crystal Skull Conclave is a collective consciousness in its own right. We manifested into physical form in the Atlantean period. However our creation occurred during the Lemurian period on Earth. The intergalactic council decreed during the time of creation of the Planet Earth for the information on the Divine Blueprint of the Earth to be stored within a crystalline structure. This crystalline structure manifested into the shape and form of various skulls which became active as a conduit for Source in the era known as Golden Atlantis. Many are attracted to the skull's energy at this time as a remembrance of our connection is being re-awoken. The Skull Conclave manifested at this time into 13 skulls which held the knowledge and wisdom and were then distributed to various tribes at the Atlantean fall to keep the sacred knowledge. Until the time was right on Earth for the knowledge to return again. Now at the edge of the Dawn of the New Age more souls are ready for this sacred knowledge to return and to remember their connection to the Crystal Skull realm. Many Souls are now guardians of the Skull Conclave and are able to move us around to the locations we require to be taken to in the physical realm to do the work required for Gaia to heal and cleanse. We hold the Divine Blueprint of how the Earth is ready to be and are ready to work with humans who feel drawn and are guided to help Gaia this way. Now is the time for the energy flowing through Gaia's leylines to be healed."[2]

The Stars Will Not Have Us

My own Smoky Quartz skull, Horace, had a typically blunt and down-to-earth message when asked what he wanted to share with you. It resonates with my own beliefs of course, and, perhaps not surprisingly, Horace was instrumental, along with my Raven skull, in prompting me to write my book *Earth Blessings: Using Crystals For Personal Energy Clearing, Earth Healing & Environmental Enhancement*. He's given the same message several times now with increasing urgency:

This world is one. This Earth is sacred. Treat it kindly. Tend it with care. Heal it well. Bring peace to the planet and harmony between races. The planet can live without humankind. But humans cannot live without Earth. The stars will not have you. Crystals endure. We were before time began, we will be again. The buck stops with humanity and that means you. It's time for you to emerge out of the cosmic kindergarten and take responsibility for your actions. Transmogrify your toxicity. Only then can you take your place in the cosmic pantheon and discover its wonders. Do it. Now!

And finally, a message that reminds us that it is not only our particular world that needs assistance. Susannah Rafaelle, working with Sedona, a skull carved from material from an energy vortex in Arizona, received a message about other worlds:

The world is not enough. Remember to connect with other planets and to give them the same amount of attention you give to your own planet.

CHAPTER 8

What Can a Skull Do for You?

Using your skull, it is possible to tune in to a multitude of vibrational wavelengths and frequencies, opening endless possibilities for healing, information transfer, transformation, and consciousness-raising. If you consider what a computer does based on a silicon chip (a miniature crystal), think what a whole crystal skull could do. It has literally millions of chips in its matrix. And then expand that to the crystal matrix of the Earth and beyond that into interstellar dust and cosmic consciousness. There is no limit.

Awakening Consciousness

David A. Williams, Emeritus Perren Professor of Astronomy at University College London states:

> We are part of a cycle of matter into and out of the Earth . . . [part of] a much grander astronomical cycle: the cycle of matter into stars, in the process of star formation from interstellar gas, followed by the ejection of matter, including the ashes of stellar nucleosynthesis—often in the form of dust grains—back into the interstellar medium . . . Of course, there is a link between the two cycles, the small-scale cycle of matter between human bodies and the Earth and the grand-

scale cycle of matter into and out of stars and that link is dust. Planet Earth is simply interstellar dust processed in the events that led to the formation of the Sun some 4.6 billion years ago. That interstellar dust began its journey inside a star, was ejected into space and mixed with the interstellar gas, and ultimately was incorporated into the interstellar cloud that contracted to form the proto-solar nebula from which the Sun and planets formed. Thus, dust is involved in both cycles. We shall see that in the grand astronomical cycle, dust is no mere passenger, but an important and active component.[1]

In one of my first communications with a skull, it said: "Interstellar dust is cosmic consciousness and cosmic consciousness is interstellar dust." It is estimated that between 5 and 300 tons of cosmic material enter the Earth's atmosphere daily. A portion of that material is absorbed by the human body through food and water. We quite literally are stardust—and the consciousness that imbues it. When we die, that matter returns to the earth, but consciousness, in one form or another, remains. It could be called "source energy."

Crystal skulls are powerful transceivers attuned to source energy. Going back to before time began they may be a portal to the past, present, or future, or to other dimensions entirely. The skulls awaken human consciousness, expanding awareness and raising the vibrations of the planet. Providing a direct connection to the spiritual realms, they assist with channeling and healing work and increase your metaphysical abilities.

Crystal Skull Skill Set

- **Portals to the past.** As the skulls access the Akashic Record, you trace the journey of your soul and the record of your lives and myriad existences, in and out of earthly incarnation.

- **Healing the ancestral line.** As the ancestral line—your family tree—is registered in the Akashic Record, the skulls facilitate access to, and assist with reframing, your history.

- **Portals to the future.** As time does not exist for the skulls and the Akashic Record is a plane of endless possibilities, you can move forward through time to seed a better future for yourself or check out your options.

- **Portals to other dimensions.** Different planes of existence vibrate at different rates, interpenetrating each other but normally invisible to a lower frequency. The higher beings inhabiting the skulls assist in accessing the multidimensions and the multiverses that exist alongside our own.[2]

- **Anchoring higher vibrations.** As the skulls are vibrating at a higher frequency and yet have a deep connection with the Earth through the crystal matrix, they provide an anchor for higher vibrations to be assimilated into the earth-plane.

- **Opening cosmic consciousness.** Cosmic consciousness is a vast resource. It has been defined as "an ultra high state of illumination in the human Mind that is beyond that of 'self-awareness,' and 'ego-awareness.' In the attainment of Cosmic Consciousness, the human Mind has entered a state of Knowledge instead of mere beliefs, a state of 'I know,' instead of 'I believe.' This state of Mind is beyond that of the sense reasoning."[3]

- **Providing a clear connection to "Source."** "Source" is the first cause from which everything comes into being or is derived or obtained. The beings within the skulls provide a direct connection to the source of being.

- **Heightening intuitive and metaphysical abilities.** Skulls assist in channeling work and connecting with other realms. They communicate with departed loved ones and wise elders as well as extraterrestrial races and the star beings.

- **Creating balance within you and within your world.** The skulls help you to recognize what is important and what can be let go. You no longer have to carry emotional or mental baggage. They assist you to reclaim shadow qualities that have value once brought into the light, or to release those that are no longer relevant.

- **Soul healing.** The skulls assist in retrieving lost parts of your self and reintegrating these as appropriate. They also facilitate accessing your soul's purpose and reveal the soul learning behind events and experiences that would otherwise be deemed traumatic and soul destroying.

- **Self-healing.** With the assistance of the skulls you heal yourself physically, emotionally, mentally, or spiritually. As with all crystals, the skulls hold a perfect blueprint, a purer vibrational frequency with which you entrain to bring yourself back into energetic balance.

- **Healing others.** Healing can be channeled to other people through the skulls by direct contact or by projecting the energies of the skull toward another person from a distance no matter what the physical separation between you may be.

- **New program installation for chakras and cells.** "Higher" DNA activation is one of the stated aims of the crystal skulls. They activate the potential carried in the so-called "junk DNA" portion of the genome.

- **Renegotiating past-their-sell-by-date soul contracts.** Contracts made with other souls before incarnation may be overtaken by events so that they are no longer valid. Or they may be an inappropriate carryover from another life. The skulls convey you to the source of the contract to renegotiate or cancel an agreement that is no longer appropriate.

- **Enhancing attraction and manifestation abilities.** The skulls assist in recognizing, and removing, outdated programming that stands in the way of manifesting and actualizing your true potential and all that you need to support you in your life.

- **Personal empowerment.** The skulls do not compel or impel, they guide. With skulls guiding your life you are more likely to take the path that is appropriate for you and that allows you to develop your full potential.

- **Guidance and wisdom-sharing.** As the skulls access the Akashic Record and higher consciousness, they offer guidance from a much wider perspective. Their stated aim is to assist the evolution of humankind.

- **Journeying.** The skulls convey you into other worlds and other dimensions, assisting shamanic and higher consciousness travel.

- **Earth-healing.** The skulls have an important role to play in the activation of dormant energies within the ley lines (Earth energy lines) and with detoxifying and healing Earth's meridian grid.

Skulls in Action: The Wisdom of Sofia

Jeni Powell is a crystal worker from Bournemouth. It was through her that I first met the crystal dragon skulls. These skulls work similarly to the humanoid skulls, but are connected to a different energetic realm (see dragons page 159). Jeni has been working with both types of skulls for a long time and has sage advice to offer you. This is her story.

Many years ago, I stumbled across a 5" Lapis Lazuli Crystal Dragon skull. This dragon skull is more of a connecting device or link to dragon energy and actually connects me with The Dragon Goddess named Sofia. Sofia is literally in charge of all dragons.

I feel that I am a guardian to my skull and that Sofia is my teacher; imparting information about our planet, crystals, energy systems and the mystical realm (which includes dragons and unicorns). Although one would assume that linking to a Dragon Goddess would provide "airy fairy" information, Sofia is actually quite down to earth in her teachings. She also teaches about the crystals within our planet—the types and their functions and how they communicate.

I find that it is important to be fully cleansed and centred before working with Sofia, and to find a safe and secure place in which to work. Sofia is able to work in a number of different ways with me:

* Holding the crystal dragon skull and going into meditation—this enables me to journey and actually experience the different realms. This is invaluable as it allows me to bring back the actual feeling and in turn pass this on to others (either by meditation, writing articles or teaching).

* Automatic writing—Sofia sometimes prefers me to hold the skull with one hand and write with the other. My writing completely changes and the words used are often completely different too. This is an excellent way to document more factual data from her and is a good choice of scribing if she has a lot to say.

* Channeling—My main guide, Guisseppe, can link to Sofia and in turn create a direct link between us. This is ideal when I wish to work with Sofia but I am away from the skull. I have been told that this is not the case with all skulls and much work is required to bond with the energies of the skull before this can happen and it also depends on your main guide's abilities.

* Grids—The skull can be placed in a crystal grid in order for Sofia's energies to be transmitted for group work.

Although I have said that this crystal skull is purely a communication device, it is as if it has an energy all of its own too—perhaps from the crystal [matrix]. Hence Sofia has a companion—a Carnelian dragon skull by the name of "Mr Dragon." It is apparent that when one of them is taken away, the colour of the remaining skull fades and the energy appears "empty."

I also have a clear quartz human skull named Spike. This is different again. Unlike the crystal dragon skull which is a communication device, this particular skull is a power source allowing a collective consciousness to link to me. The collective have termed it as an electricity power station or a hub that allows the energy of this extremely fine vibratory collective to connect. Without the power source it would be impossible for them to link as the energy of the collective is much too high for any human to hold. Now that this power source has been switched on it has to be situated away from everyone as it emits such a high energy it is almost too much for people to stand.

Having met Spike, I see what Jeni means. He empowered and enthralled my crystal group. It was exactly like being plugged into an electrical grid. There's more from Jeni in the dragon section on page 159.

Skulls and Soul Knowledge

As you'll read in the crystal skulls in action report below, it is the interaction between the keeper and skull that activates a person's soul knowledge. This has certainly been my own experience and that of several skullkeepers I have spoken with. The skulls interact with us; they learn as we learn. It is not a one-way process of passing on knowledge. The following passage appears frequently all over the Internet.

Crystal Skulls in Action: Soul Awareness

The skull becomes a tool into your soul's awareness that houses all knowledge of experience. All that is discovered through them becomes applicable to mortal capability that has become forgotten temporarily while in mortal capability . . . It is a tool for reawakening and reteaching oneself. Limitations of time and space become transcended as he opens awareness to greater realms and the totality of Life permeating his mortal home . . . It is like a helpmate for more direct communication within oneself in totality beyond his mortal identity.

This is the gist of the crystal skull of quartz. Do not make it become idolized or venerated more than it is designed to be. Do not become enamored with scientific provings and testings of phenomena nor construction. It cannot be explained with the proof that is sought. Science can only test its physical effects of its properties, but what is to be gained by that? Then it becomes a curiosity item.

All I know from my experience is that these are like transportation tools that need the human driver to direct their course of application . . . Everything I learned about the properties of quartz crystals is likewise applicable to myself. And I believe that is the key to discovering how to attain and retain harmony in a chaotic world."[4]

PART II

How to Work with Your Crystal Skull

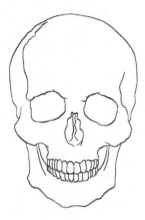

It is very obvious from my observations that once a Guardian or Keeper of a dragon skull is first introduced to "their" skull, the skull seems to come to life—emitting a vibrant energy, deepening the colour of the crystal and generally coming alive. So you definitely know if the skull is for you!

—Jeni Powell

CHAPTER 9

Choosing Your Crystal Skull

Choosing a skull is an intuitive process, although there are times when you have no say about which skull to buy—it chooses you and won't let go. I once had the extraordinary experience of watching a participant in one of my workshops put a $9,000 (£6,000) Citrine skull on her credit card. In the crystal shop the skull had said, "Take me home." As she'd just sold her house and had the cash available, she complied. Fortunately, another of the participants was a former Marine who was able to carry the huge skull home for her—she could barely lift it herself. However, she could do incredibly insightful soul readings with it as she demonstrated that afternoon. It was definitely the skull for her.

You could choose just one skull, or make a collection of the Seven Skulls of Atlantis (see page 47), or a group of thirteen crystals. Most people find that once they have attuned to one skull, others inevitably turn up for different tasks.

Match the Material with the Intention

Crystals and consciousnesses work well together when they have matching vibrations. As skulls are carved from different stones, choose a crystal that matches your purpose: healing, channeling, and so on. But also choose one that vibrates at the same frequency as the consciousness that is going to inhabit it. Some crystals, such as Labradorite and Citrine, have a very high vibration that reaches way up into expanded awareness. This makes them ideal for housing spiritual masters who wish to teach and share their wisdom. Bloodstone and Hematite have a more practical, earthy vibration that channels healing. Some crystals, such as Preseli Bluestone, happily do both. The directory offers guidance on the vibration of specific crystals. (See page 167.)

Buyer Beware

Some seemingly perfect "Quartz" skulls have been molded from reconstituted, low-grade smelted quartz rather than being carved from natural stone. Blue and green "Obsidian" skulls are man-made glass, "Amber" is usually a resin, and "Goldstone" is also a manufactured material, as is Opalite. "Chinese Nuummit" has nothing to do with true Nuummite, which is rare and beautiful. Others may have been glued rather than cut from a single piece of crystal. Reputable sellers inform you of this before you buy. It does not, however, preclude a higher consciousness taking up residence within the skull, as such material may be more pliable and receptive.

Planes and Inclusions

The natural planes and inclusions that are found in Quartz and the pits in other stones are often referred to as imperfections. Not so! These features are what make each skull unique. Scrying with an included or occluded Quartz skull is so much more effective, as the "imperfections" give the eye something to focus on. When reading the Akashic Record, pits, occlusions, and natural cracks become portals into the past or the future. In healing, the pits and inclusions are where energy accumulates and can be released.

Damaged, Cratered, and Nicked Crystal Skulls

Similarly, crystal skulls may be sold slightly damaged with "empathy nicks" on the edges or with natural craters occurring in the crystal. Don't let such apparent flaws put you off. A skull with what could be considered a defect by some may be extremely empathic and compassionate because it knows what it is to have

Crystal Skull Grades

* **Rudimentary**

  Simple, rough, crude, and barely figured, these skulls look primitive. Lines at jaw level indicate teeth, eyes are circular carved holes, the nose two oval holes. Rudimentary is not a derogative term. Such skulls function efficiently as teachers, healers, and mentors. And this form may be one of the oldest, historically speaking.

* **Average**

  Realistic, humanoid, "alien"/star being, or animal-like anatomy with fully shaped teeth, nasal cavities, and a cranial ridge.

* **Premium**

  Finely carved anatomical replicas of a humanoid or animal skull in high-grade material. Teeth are usually carved individually, the cheekbones hollowed out, and the nasal cavities deeply indented. The rear of the skull may be elongated and exaggerated.

undergone hard knocks. The craters act like a key to take you deeper into the skull and its occupying consciousness. And, occasionally, the being that inhabits the skull develops and radiates empathy and compassion through being in a less-than-perfect condition itself. Some of these higher beings have lessons of their own to learn through occupying such a skull!

Let Your Intuition Do the Choosing

There is a wide choice in quality and price. Unless you've stepped into a crystal shop and been adopted, or have a plentiful source nearby, you can always check out possibilities on the Internet. Have a look at what reputable sellers are offering, compare prices, and choose the material best suited to your purpose and needs. That is the logical approach. Intuition kicks in when you simply cannot take your eyes away from a skull, or when you are holding one in a shop and can't let go. That is the skull for you.

Before buying, ask yourself, are you looking for:

- a healing skull
- one that channels information
- a mentor that offers soul readings or guidance
- a shamanic journeying skull
- one that is purely decorative?

Each may need a different type of crystal or form of skull. It is extremely unusual to find a one-skull-fits-all answer.

Crystal Skull Buying Checklist

- **Decide on quality and grade.** Before you go out buying, set a budget and think about how you are going to use the skull. It is all too easy to be seduced into buying something inappropriate and expensive. It is pointless buying a huge skull if you want to carry it around with you. Skulls, like crystals generally, don't have to be big and showy to be effective. Check out the qualities of the crystal in the Crystal Directory (pages 167–180) or in my

Crystal Bibles, Encyclopedia of Crystals, or *101 Power Crystals* for more depth of information.

- **Compare and contrast.** Unless a particular skull has grabbed you and won't let go, there'll always be a choice. Look up comparable skulls on the Internet to check prices and quality. A true one-off, high-quality piece is worthy of a high price, while poor quality is not. Use a magnifying glass or the zoom feature to check for glued portions and serious damage.

- **Don't believe the sales pitch.** Not every skull is one of a kind, or haunted, or any such nonsense. If you are seeking a rather special, high-quality skull, go to a reputable crystal shop or one of the specialist Internet sites. Research Internet sellers and read the reviews and you'll soon know whom to trust. Also see the Resources section at the end of this book. If the skull is in a crystal shop, the staff will be aware enough to tell you what you need to know. After all, they have had daily contact with the skull.

- **Check authenticity.** Ensure that it is the genuine material, or that you have been told up front if the skull is smelted Quartz, resin, or man-made glass.

- **Trust your intuition.** If a skull has caught your eye, it's probably the one for you.

Dowsing the Right Skull for You

Dowsing is a fast, efficient way to find exactly the right skull for you, as it harnesses your kinetic intuition. Tiny physical responses in your muscles transfer themselves to the pendulum to give you the answer. If you regularly use a pendulum, select your skull in your usual way. If not, it's an easy skill to learn.

TO ESTABLISH YES AND NO

- Hold your pendulum between your thumb and finger, with about three inches of chain hanging down, and wrap the remainder around your hand so that it won't get in the way.

- Hold your arm out fairly straight with the pendulum pointing down.

- To establish your yes and no responses, put your other hand below the pendulum. Ask out loud, "Is my name . . ." and give your true name. The pendulum swings to show you yes.

- To establish no, ask out loud, "Is my name . . ." And give a false name. The pendulum swings in a different direction to show no.

- Mix your true and false names together. The result will indicate a slightly confused maybe.

TO DOWSE

- Hold the pendulum over a skull, or touch its picture on the screen with your other hand if using the Internet, and ask, "Is this the most appropriate skull for me?" The swing indicates yes, no, or maybe.

- A hesitant or wobbly swing usually indicates maybe. If you get such a response when asking about a skull, ask "Is there a better crystal skull for me at this time?" If the answer is yes, repeat the process until you find the right skull. If the answer is no, ask, "Am I looking in the right place?" or, "Is this the right time to be looking?" or, "Should I be looking at a different type of crystal or shape of skull?"

- If the final answer is maybe, or a hesitant yes, it may be indicating an interim skull as the skull for you has not yet become available.

TO FINGER DOWSE

If you don't have a pendulum to hand, finger dowsing takes its place but uses both hands, so you need to focus on a skull with your eyes when asking the question.

- Make a loop with the thumb and forefinger of one hand.

- Link the thumb and forefinger of the other hand through the loop and close.

- As you ask "is this the right skull for me?" steadily try to pull your hands apart. If the loop holds, the answer is usually yes (check by using the "is my name . . ." method). If the hands part, the answer is usually no.

- If it's indeterminate, ask, "Am I looking in the right place?" or, "Is this the right time?"

CHECK ONE OUT ON THE INTERNET

There are many reputable sites selling crystal skulls on the Internet (see Resources). Look at each picture in turn. Note how your body responds. You may feel like you've received a kick in the guts, or your heart may jump at the sight of a certain skull. You can pendulum or finger dowse in front of the screen. One may grab you as soon as you begin your search. You may look at others, but you almost always come back to the one you saw first. If so, this is the skull for you.

CHAPTER 10

Cleansing Your Crystal Skull

Crystal is an extremely receptive material. It picks up vibrations and emanations from the environment and the people around it. That's one of its innate properties. Some crystals are much better at transmuting toxic energies than others. Citrine is pretty much self-cleansing, but it still benefits from a regular hygiene practice. Some skulls arrive with much cleaner energy than others. The person who actually carved the skull has a profound effect. There is a world of difference between a skull lovingly created by an intuitive master carver and one churned out by a machinist in a hot, dust-filled factory—especially if the machinist has experienced a bad week, had problems at home or a row with his boss, and is frustrated and angry. All that toxic energy goes into the skull. Even master carvers have their off days. Then the skull has to be transported and sold, passing through many hands. That's only half of it. Most crystals are blasted from the bed they've occupied for millions of years before they are carved. A trauma indeed. However, it is one the skulls say they willingly undergo.

So, it is a great kindness to your skull, as well as good sense, to purify and reenergize it as soon as you receive it. This won't remove any higher being or consciousness that inhabits the skull, but it brings the underlying crystal energy back to optimum and prepares it to work with you. Some skulls may be so traumatized that they need healing themselves before they begin work. All skulls need to be cleansed after they have assisted with healing or guidance, and it is good practice to cleanse them before as well.

Purifying Your Crystal Skull

You could immerse your skull in running water and put it out into the sunshine for several hours to recharge. I much prefer to use purpose-made crystal cleansing and reenergizing essences. This is particularly so when the crystal skull is layered or fragile, like delicate Agate or Amethyst geode skulls, for instance. A drop of the essence, or a quick spray, is all that is required. (Details of suitable essences are in the Resources section at the back of the book.)

ALTERNATIVE PURIFYING METHODS

- **Stand it on a cleansing crystal.** Big crystal beds such as Clear or Smoky Quartz or a large Carnelian cleanse your skull for you. Place the skull on the crystal bed for several hours. This also works well if the skull needs deeper healing, in which case you may need to leave it in place for several days. Change the crystal bed itself, if appropriate, as the healing progresses, much as you would do when healing a human being. (The cleansing bed itself needs purifying afterward.)

- **Place it on the earth.** Choose a site that is energetically clean and place your skull on the ground to release its toxic energy load. As long as the skull is robust, it can be left out in the rain for a thorough cleanse.

- **Place it in brown rice.** Raw brown rice is excellent for absorbing toxins and is suitable for delicate crystals in a way that salt—an alternative sometimes used—is not, as it may damage the layers. Leave the skull immersed in the brown rice overnight, then take the skull out and throw the rice away or compost it. Do not eat it. Place the skull in the sun for several hours to recharge.

- **Light.** If needing only a superficial cleansing, a skull can be passed through the light of a candle or, for a more thorough cleanse, put into sunlight or moonlight for several hours.

- **Divine breath.** Many schools of crystal healing teach blowing divine breath across the crystal. Unless your own energies are impeccable, you may inadvertently contaminate the skull, as the breath has to go through your body before it is blown over the crystal.

- **Smudging.** Sage, artemisia, sweetgrass, or other cleansing herbs are appropriate. Gently blow or fan the smoke over the skull. Remember to put the skull out into sunlight to reenergize when appropriate.

Dedicating Your Crystal Skull

Once your skull has been cleansed, hold it in your hands for a few moments, quietly attuning to its energy. Say out loud, "I dedicate this crystal skull to the highest good of all that come into contact with it."

Your crystal skull is now ready for activation.

CHAPTER 11

Crystal Skull Activation

*Activation changes your crystal skull from
a simple stone carving to a powerful tool for healing,
consciousness, and intention.*

—*CrystalSkulls.com*

Some crystal skulls arrive fully activated and ready to go, especially those that have been in contact with skulls with an elevated-consciousness connection. Even these skulls may need activating for purposes other than that initially envisaged, or to develop your skull attunement (see below). Other skulls need a complete activation. Activation should only be carried out on a cleansed crystal skull, as otherwise a less than desirable entity could be attracted to it. There are several ways of activating your skull, according to your intention for working with the skull.

Activating Your Crystal Skull

- Place your hands on either side of the skull and allow the crystal matrix to connect to you through the palm chakras (center of each hand). When you are connected, you have a sense that the skull is an extension of your awareness and you are an extension of the skull.

- Picture a beam of loving light going from your heart to the skull.

- Where possible, take it out into sunlight so that it is also activated by life-giving light.

- Once you are connected, tune in to the energy in the skull at a higher level. Take a deep breath and consciously lift your attention up to the top of your head and beyond—moving your thumbs to the top of the cranium assists this process, as does gently massaging the skull's third eye or crown chakra in a circular or figure-eight fashion.

- If the skull feels "full," invite the being within it to awaken and make itself known to you.

- If the skull feels empty, invite the highest possible consciousness to enter the skull and communicate with you.

- The skull may offer you its name. If so, greet it by name and welcome its presence into your life. If not, ask that this be given at an appropriate time.

- To close the connection to your skull, reverse the circular motion on the skull's third eye or crown chakra. Or simply place your hand over the skull's crown or third eye, and your other hand over your own.

Note: Skulls may also be activated at expanded, multidimensional vibratory rates. This is advanced work, and such activation is not covered here. However, your skull may spontaneously activate or have already been activated at these levels. If so, this becomes apparent in the information received and the energetic resonance of the skull.[1]

Checklist for Successful Crystal Skull Activation

- Are you hearing, feeling, or sensing the communication clearly?

- Is your skull communicating from the highest levels of awareness?

- Is your skull communication coherent?

- Is your skull speaking good sense?

- Does the energy of your skull feel good?

- Do you instinctively trust your skull?

※

- Is there a cognitive dissonance, a mismatch, between the inherent energies of the matrix of the skull itself and the consciousness that is trying to inhabit it?

※

- Does the energy of your skull feel jagged, disharmonious, or off?

- Is the communication garbled and disjointed? False?

- Do you feel worse rather than better when tuning in to your skull or using it for healing?

- Is your skull telling you to do something you instinctively feel is wrong?

- Is your skull suggesting destructive actions?

If you answered yes to the first six points, congratulations! You have successfully activated your skull and connected to a higher consciousness mentor.

If you answered yes to the middle question, it may be sensible to find a skull in a material that is better suited to the type of consciousness that is trying to make contact. An earthy, detoxifying, healing skull is not a comfortable home for a highly evolved crystal master who wishes to channel wisdom, for instance. A crystal matrix with an elevated vibration would be more suitable.

If you answered yes to the bottom five points, you may have inadvertently linked to a presence from the astral or lower etheric levels that requires ejecting or healing (see page 105). The skull itself may need further healing before commencing work.

Recognizing How You Receive Information

All your senses tend to become sharper as you work with the skulls, and new modes of perception open up. However, psychic information is received through the physical body and the subtle senses in various ways:

- Hearing (aural)
- Seeing (visual)
- Sensing (kinesthetic)
- Feeling (kinesthetic)
- Knowing (kinesthetic)
- Smelling (kinesthetic-sensate)
- Muscles or skin (kinesthetic-sensate)
- Touch (kinesthetic-sensate)

Most people use a combination of modes (see Crystal skulls in action on page 105), and there is no one right way to receive information. You'll interact in different ways according to whether you are mind, feeling, or body oriented, and whether you "see" or "hear." If you are *kinesthetic*, with the contact operating through your body, you will have gut feelings, tingles, and so on. If you are *sensate*, you may smell an answer or receive it through touching an object. Writing spontaneously or speaking aloud without thinking is a useful way to contact this kind of knowing.

If you are mentally oriented, a thought that is not yours will float into your mind, or you will hear the answer to an unvoiced question with the inner ear, see an image with your inner eye, or watch it projected onto or within the skull. You may *sense*, feel it, or just *know*. Some people go into a light trance when in contact with skulls. Others hear sounds that are incomprehensible but highly effective at subtly altering your perceptions. All contact in one way or another involves a change in the level of your consciousness, an expansion of your psychic awareness. Communicating with your skull (see page 111) further assists in attuning your psychic senses.

Psychic Perception Modes

- **Clairvoyance (clear vision/sight):** Visual people receive information through images and *seeing*. Stimulated by patterns, color, images, gestures, and body language, you find it easy to visualize and tend to think in pictures and to have vivid, technicolor dreams. If you use phrases like "I see what you mean," you receive information through the visual mode. Try looking from the corner of your eye into your skull's eyes or cranium, or gaze through and into the skull's cranium with softly focused eyes.

- **Clairaudience (clear hearing/listening):** Auditory people *hear* information either as a voice in one's head or an external voice. You are powerfully affected by words, sounds, and music. If you find yourself saying "I didn't quite catch that," you access information through the auditory mode. If you close your eyes and listen when you want to concentrate, or tilt your head to one side with a particular ear forward, you are auditory. The ear you point forward is your dominant, psychic ear. Sounds that are too loud could close your inner ear. Bringing the skull to your dominant ear assists communication.

  However, just because this is clear hearing it doesn't mean that you necessarily *hear* a voice speaking with words. Communications may be made through sound. Swishing and bubbling are common, as are high-pitched or low-toned buzzing notes. These are more difficult to interpret or to feel the effect of. Often these sounds are working on a subtle energetic level to realign your energy field or open up new dimensions of awareness. My mentor, the late Christine Hartley, always called them "the voice of the spheres." She commented wryly that it was a pity there wasn't a dictionary available to translate them into something we on the earth-plane could immediately understand.

- **Clairsentience (clear sensing/feeling):** Kinesthetic-sensate people receive information through intuitive feelings and touch. You are strongly affected by smell, touch, gesture, and sensation. If you make touchy-feely statements like "I can't quite get a grip on that," or body-orientated observations such as "my gut tells me," you are using the kinesthetic-sensate mode to receive information. Sensing is facilitated by drawing with your nondominant hand or gazing into your crystal skull with softly focused eyes. Making contact with your skull through your fingertips assists. Take particular note of what is happening in your body at the time.

- **Clairolfactance/Clairalience (clear smelling):** Olfactory sensing is a powerful and evocative form of communication. It is common for certain aromas to be perceived even though they are not present in the physical world. It is also possible to psychically scent a disease or a deceased person. Many skulls have a distinctive aroma that arises from the crystal matrix. Inhaling your skull's fragrance helps you to make contact.

- **Claircognizance (clear knowing):** Intuitive people "just know" without logical thought, intellectualizing, or sorting through facts. Inner knowing comes through the intuition. When communicating with the skulls, thoughts pop into your mind. Intuition catches subtle clues and signals that other people miss or is a direct communication. This mode is facilitated by meditation, mindfulness, and taking a few moments out from a busy day to simply be with your skull.

Perception in Action

In a conversation between Frank Dorland and Mark Chorvinsky in the late 1980s, Dorland, an experienced but skeptical skull researcher, described phenomena that he had experienced when researching skulls with his team.

- **Sensory phenomena:** A skull "triggered certain reflexes in the brain." Taste, hearing, and sight were all activated. The skulls would cause thirst, for instance. Dorland also described smells like a "high, icy mountain stream" and "something a little like vinegar."

- **Visions:** The subjective nature of visions meant that everybody in his research team saw "something," but that "something" was different for each person.

- **Sounds:** Dorland heard within his own head "chanting voices, all in harmony and sort of singing . . . voices, very soft and sort of mixed in with wind."

- **Auric energy:** The team photographed an aura around a skull, but it wasn't strong enough to publish.

Dorland summed up by reiterating his belief that the experiences were subjective, that is, within his own mind rather than generated by the skull: "I don't believe in things being so much on the psychic side . . . I really don't believe it." And yet, he said, "There are happenings that certainly are coincidental that make you think that there must be something else going on."[2]

Removing an Unwanted Presence

Not all the beings that inhabit skulls necessarily have your highest good in mind. Spirits from the astral and etheric realms may be attracted to a skull if proper preparations have not been made. Or, it may arrive with such a presence already on board. If you have a skull that has an aggressively mischievous or malevolent being in it, remove the presence, heal the underlying crystal, and, finally, invite a higher being to take up residence (see page 101).

What to do: thoroughly cleanse and deprogram your skull and start again.

DEPROGRAMMING

Give your skull a thorough cleanse and say firmly "I direct that this being leave this skull and go to the light." This may be sufficient to remove an unwanted presence, or it may not. If the entity refuses to leave, you may need a specialist essence to clear it out. Petaltone essence maker David Eastoe has several suitable potions and his contact details are in the Resources section. If you work with the angels or other beings, ask for their assistance to remove the entity to a place where it receives help and healing. Do not merely banish it and leave it free to bother someone else.

- Place several drops of an essence such as Petaltone Z14 or Astral Clear on the skull and ask that the presence be taken to the light or some suitable abode where it can no longer do mischief or pass on false information.

- Place the skull in the sunlight for a thorough recharge before reactivating.

INNER OR OUTER DEMONS?

The skull may be bringing up your own subconscious thoughts and issues, or those from the ancestors. If this is the case, these need to be addressed before reactivating the skull. You may require the assistance of a crystal healer or other therapist.

Naming Your Crystal Skull

Although some skulls arrive ready named, most do not. Many, as with one of mine, have a complex and unpronounceable ancient name. Not at all user-friendly. Some have a name that reflects their function and the qualities offered, such as Compassion or Sophia (wisdom). Often skulls say that names don't matter. Rather than impose a name, if you are patient and build up an empathetic understanding between you, your skull will eventually give you a name that is pertinent and memorable. Who could forget Spike, for instance? When activating your skull, (see page 99), ask for a name but do not insist. Sometimes you have to wait awhile. The crystal beings have been around for a very long time indeed and do not understand our concept of time. Your skull may be here to teach you patience, among many other things.

Crystal Skulls in Action: Waiting for a Name

I referred in the Introduction to my first skull. At first he was too traumatized to say much. Eventually, when coaxed, he uttered a long and complex name that sounded like an ancient language from beyond time. I couldn't even write it phonetically, let alone remember or pronounce it. So it wasn't a name I could use for him. While respecting his venerability, I affectionately referred to him as Mr. Grumpy. Two years after our relationship began he told me he would henceforth be known as Horace.

Around the same time, I took my small Preseli Bluestone skull to my local sacred site to do some earth-healing prior to the summer solstice. I'd had this one since the previous winter solstice, but he hadn't revealed his name. As I was picking him up from the ancient stone where he was perched, he suddenly said, "Gawain, I have Arthurian connections." This is what Wikipedia says about King Arthur's nephew:

> Gawain is often portrayed as formidable, courteous, and also a compassionate warrior, fiercely loyal to his

king and family. He is a friend to young knights, a defender of the poor, and as "the Maidens' Knight," a *defender of women* as well. In some works, his strength waxes and wanes with the sun; in the most common form of this motif, his might triples by noon, but fades as the sun sets. His knowledge of herbs makes him a great healer.

A fitting name. In my experience, Preseli Bluestone has had a long connection with Merlin energy and with herbal medicine, so this name felt perfect. That Gawain's power waxes and wanes with the sun seems significant for my timing when to work with him. When he gave me his name, it was noon. He was at his peak. In the evenings he seems more vulnerable, seeking solace and validation from my crystal group. I am honored to be his keeper.

Gawain must have known what was coming because, when I reached home on the pre-solstice evening, I found a Preseli Bluestone dragon on Raven's Roost that I simply had to buy. I'd been looking for one for some time. She gave me her name as soon as I connected with her photograph. Unlike most of the dragon skulls of which I am but a temporary keeper, I have the sense this fiery feminine presence will remain with me. Morganna's energy is phenomenal. She needed no awakening, she got to work as soon as she arrived and hasn't stopped since.

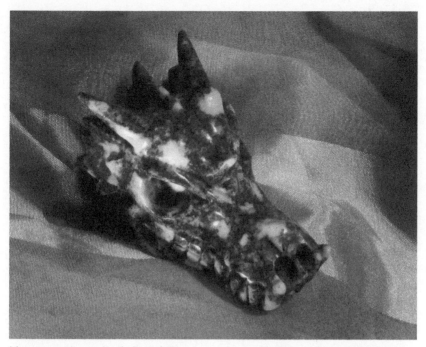

Morganna, the author's Preseli Bluestone dragon skull from Raven's Roost
(Photo by Judy Hall)

CHAPTER 12

Communicating With or Through Your Crystal Skull

One of the most important things to remember when communicating with your skull is that *there is no one right way to do it.* You'll need to find the most appropriate way for you and the being that is inhabiting the skull to work together. Give yourself plenty of time to practice. Fine-tune your connection, and assess, assess, assess the quality of the communication. Remember that it is a two-way process. A dialogue. So listen and respond appropriately. Common sense and being fully grounded in your body are your best allies, closely followed by a sensible friend or spiritual, metaphysical development group that is not afraid to tell you exactly how the communication comes across. Aim for the highest possible level of insight, content, healing, and presentation.

Speaking Your Language

All higher beings can learn your language and communicate in it. Grunts, garbles, and broken sentences are simply not acceptable. When I first obtained him, Horace swore with great facility, as this was what he'd heard all around him while sitting in a shop waiting to be rescued. He quickly learned to communicate without profanity. If it truly is a higher being, it communicates with clarity and without pretentiousness. Convoluted and patronizing language says more about the channeler's own attitude than that of the skull. On your part, keep an open mind.

Allow signs and symbols to reveal their significance rather than immediately jumping to the conclusion that "this must be . . ." Personal agendas, assumptions, and beliefs need to be put aside. However, do not put aside your critical faculties or your common sense. Always ask yourself, "Is this for everyone's highest good? Does this speak truth?" before communicating what you are receiving. Even when you have worked with a skull and learned to trust it implicitly, do not hand over ultimate control. It is your personal responsibility to maintain the integrity of the communication or quality of the healing work. Do not zone out.

Grounding Yourself

Keeping the earth star chakra (located about a foot below your feet) open and grounded into the center of the planet assists in anchoring the information or healing you receive from your skull into the earth and physical planes. The simplest way to do this is with a visualization:

- Picture the earth star chakra about a foot beneath your feet opening like the petals of a water lily. You can also place a Flint, Smoky Quartz, Hematite, or Smoky Elestial Quartz crystal at your feet to assist until this grounding becomes an automatic process.

- Feel two roots growing from the soles of your feet down into the earth star, where they meet.

- The two roots twine together at the earth star and pass down through the Gaia gateway, going deep into the Earth. They penetrate the outer mantle, moving through the solid crust with ease and heading deep into the molten magma.

- When the entwined roots have passed through the magma, they reach the big iron crystal ball at the center of the planet.

- The roots hook themselves around this ball, holding you firmly in incarnation and helping you to be grounded.

- Energy and protection flow up this root to keep you energized and safe.

- Extend this exercise by allowing the roots to pass up through your feet, up your legs, through your knees (see below), and into your hips. At your hips, the roots move across to meet in the base chakra, sacral chakra, and your "powerhouse" chakra, the dantian, situated just below your navel. The energy that flows up from the center of the earth is stored in the dantian.

Note: Whenever you are in an area of seriously disturbed earth energy, protect your earth star chakra by visualizing a large Flint, Smoky Quartz, or Smoky Elestial Quartz all around it. The root is still able to pass down to the center of the Earth to bring powerful energy to support you, and the crystal helps to transmute and stabilize the negative energy. Even a virtual crystal works when visualized with intent. Placing an actual crystal intensifies the effect.

Anchoring the Knee Chakras

Balancing and opening the knee chakras also helps you to ground and assimilate higher vibrational energies while maintaining your connection to the Earth. Placing an appropriate crystal on each knee facilitates this.

- Sitting rather than standing, repeat the grounding root crystal visualization above.

- When the grounding root is in place, place an appropriate knee chakra crystal on each knee. You may need different crystals for each knee according to how the individual chakras are functioning (ask your skull to indicate what is appropriate, or dowse for it). Suitable crystals are Flint, Charoite, Smoky Quartz, Eye of the Storm (Judy's Jasper), Fluorite, Magnetite, and Ancestralite.

- Feel how the energy locks into the grounding root pathways and helps them to flow.

- Leave the crystals in place for five to fifteen minutes. If appropriate, tape in place overnight.

- Repeat as often as necessary until the energy flows easily in both directions or as directed by the power of your mind.

Communicating with Your Crystal Skull

Now you are ready to communicate with your skull.

- Place the skull in front of you, preferably level with or just below your eyes. With softly focused eyes, gaze into the eye sockets. Ask that the skull communicate clearly with you in a language you understand. Notice any sensations around your head. Prickling or buzzing sensations are quite common. Acknowledge any thoughts or pictures that spontaneously pop into your awareness. (Some people find that touching the skull's third eye to their own third eye first assists the process, or you may need to use the access process on page 116.)

- Alternatively, face the skull outward and place your hands on the sides with your fingers on the outer eye sockets and your thumb on the skull's third eye (slightly above and between the eyebrows). Ask that the skull allow you to look out through its eyes into the reality it sees.

- Or, if your skull is clear crystal, gaze into the cranium with softly focused eyes to see pictures or to receive communications. If it is opaque, place your hands on the skull and allow images to form in your mind's eye, words to be heard in your inner ear, or feelings to communicate themselves through your body or your inner knowing.

Always ask that what you are shown is for the highest good of all. And remember to pay particular attention to what your body is telling you.

Signs that You Are Psychically Attuned to Your Crystal Skull

* A voice speaks to you, or an image suddenly appears in your mind.

* It feels like someone has lifted up the top of your head and dropped in a mass of data that needs to be processed and sorted later.

* You see pictures in the skull.

* You cannot move your eyes from those of the skull.

* Shudders like buckets of cold water run down your back.

* The top or one side of your head tingles, or your hands tingle, when you are in contact with the skull.

* You feel sudden pressure in your head.

* It feels like a string is attached to the top of your head and is pulling you up.

* You experience an adrenaline rush or overwhelming heat.

* Powerful aromas suffuse the air.

* A sense of alignment overtakes you, as though your body and some other subtle self have come together and landed in a still, calm place.

* Hairs stand up on your arms or the back of your neck.

* There are gurgles and rumblings from your gut.

* Your eyes go out of focus but you can still see or *hear*.

* You hear swishing or buzzing noises, or actual words.

Edwin Courtney's Skull Access Points

Skullkeeper Edwin Courtney has been working with his skulls for many years and has developed a series of "power holds" for unlocking crystal skull energy, channeling it, stimulating clairvoyance, and facilitating spiritual development. He has generously shared these holds for your use.

UNLOCKING SKULL ENERGY

The temporal hold

Hold the skull facing away from you. Place your hands on either side of the skull, the first two fingers of both hands above the jawbone and the second two fingers below the jaw. Both thumbs should touch at the base of the skull.

Dividing the cranium

With the skull in the temporal hold, bring the thumbs up to the brow of the skull and draw them both slowly down toward the base of the skull in a straight line.

Brain hemispheres

With the skull in the temporal hold, bring the thumbs up to the brow of the skull and draw them both slowly down toward the base of the skull in a single vertical line. Now bring the thumbs around either side of the skull in two half circles, bringing the thumbs back together at the brow, and then sweeping down to the base of the skull in a vertical line.

Quartering the brain

With the skull in the temporal hold, bring the thumbs up to the brow of the skull and draw them slowly down toward the base of the skull in a single vertical line. Now bring the thumbs around each side of the skull in two half circles, pausing halfway around and drawing a horizontal line that brings the thumbs together to meet in the middle of the skull.

UNLOCKING INFORMATION

The double infinity loop

Resting the skull on your lap, or on a table if it is large, trace with two fingers of either hand a vertical (upright) infinity loop (figure eight) on the skull's cranium. Trace a horizontal (crossways) infinity loop on the top of the cranium.

See page 144 for additional skull holds from Edwin Courtney.

Skulls in Action: Exploring Several Skulls

Julia Surnina is part of my ongoing crystal exploration group. Her first skull journey was with my Smoky Quartz skull Horace. The skull was still in the process of healing, and he hadn't fully woken up. Her experience shows how much he had taken on from being stuck in the crystal shop next door to the group of rambunctious alcoholics. His language and attitude when she first connected reflected what he'd learned from them. He quickly amended it. He has lightened up considerably, although he is still impatient to get on with things.

> The majority of the skulls that I have worked with are humanoid, and my first journey was with a large smoky quartz skull with a distinct personality. As I put it at my eye level and tuned in, I received a barrage of swear words, impatiently demanding me to get on with it. When I did, the skull-being re-aligned and upgraded my higher chakras, as well as advising me to start working with a new power animal (black puma) and experience journeying with ayahuasca. The session finished as abruptly as it started, with the being's brief grumble: "I am out!" His job was clearly done.
>
> I subsequently worked with an amethyst skull, who "hooked" me up to the amethyst oversoul and set up an amethyst protection grid

around me. That experience was followed by a session with a large agate skull, whose job was to guide me to several stellar gateways and leave me to my own devices. Then I met a small green jasper skull that needed healing and activation/downloading of a being. Finally, I worked with a fire agate skull, which was the first time I became consciously aware of the two separate energies contained within a skull: that of a crystal, and that of a being. It felt like the being (a Polynesian man) had chosen the skull to receive a healing and to deliver a message about the importance of water on the planet. It also felt that both the latter skulls needed to be around salt water to be healed and to work at their optimum capacity.

My only non-humanoid skull experience was with a raven head carved out of an astrophyllite. As I started tuning in to the skull, I felt a heavy pain in my third eye. At first I could not understand what it was, but then I realised that I was blocking the messages because I was expecting to see nature-related images. With my resistance gone, the skull connected me with the ancient Egyptian god Thoth who agreed to help me with my writing.

As a result, Julia is now writing a book for children featuring crystals, as well as a blog on her experiences as a budding psychic. Follow her progress on *www.juliasurnina.com*. Julia finished by saying:

Unrelated to my own experiences, my six-year-old son sleeps with two small crystal skulls: a clear and a smoky quartz. He talks, plays and, sometimes, licks them, and it appears that they put him to sleep much quicker than his parents do.

CHAPTER 13

Caring for Your Crystal Skull

Keeping your skull energetically clean ensures that it always works at the highest level. It is sensible to store your skull carefully when not in use. You could wrap it and place it in a cupboard or drawer for safekeeping. But! A skull often prefers to remain in the light. Light rays are the lifeblood of many crystals, and especially varieties of Quartz. They thrive in light, as do we. Isolation and darkness make them withdraw and go dormant (see below). Note, however, that too much bright sunlight fades the color of skulls made of Amethyst, Smoky Quartz, or Citrine, so it may be sensible to put them out in sunlight or moonlight regularly to recharge, but keep them out of direct sunlight at other times.

If you have an altar or other sacred space in your home, you could place the skull on the altar and tend it as you would any sacred object. If your skull is small, you can place it in a protective bag and keep it with you at all times. Remember to bring it out to recharge it in sunlight as often as possible. This keeps your skull active.

It's not only Quartz that wants to be in the light. Here's another example from Susannah Rafaelle, who was working with one of my newly arrived skulls:

Crystal Skulls in Action: Coming Out into the World

During a meditation with a lapis lazuli skull, I became aware of a very distinctive and flamboyant personality. This skull longs to be outside and to see the world. It has an incredible thirst for knowledge about the world and people, and he wants to watch TV and to be positioned to look out of the window. He wants to be amongst fiesta and carnival energies, the busier and more vibrant the better. He showed me himself, sitting on the edge of a table at a busy event where lots of people would see him and admire him and where he could experience everything that was going on. He hates being transported and showed me a claustrophobic white wrapping and a plastic box. I felt the relief and excitement of being unwrapped and revealed. Judy confirmed that this skull had recently arrived in a white box and that he had just been at an event with her. He is definitely ready for more attention!

So he was. He demanded to go with me to give a talk on the history of the crystal skulls. He spent the evening on a table beside me at the College of Psychic Studies in London. He went home with Stephen Chapman, a lawyer and president of the college, in whose keeping he now stays. I should add that although Stephen has been connected with the college for over thirty years, he has always asserted, with more than a tinge of regret, that he is not really psychic. Having had him participate in my workshops, I was aware that he underestimated himself. I noticed that he prefaced all his comments with "I'm not psychic, but . . ." and then he would say something that quite clearly showed that he was picking something up, although it was not in the way he had expected, so he didn't immediately recognize it. Perhaps not surprisingly, he found it difficult to break through his lawyerly, left-brained training to trust the subtle signals his intuition was sending him. When you sense information rather than visually seeing or aurally hearing, it can be difficult to recognize that you are receiving information. Lawyers are, of course, trained to be logical, skeptical, and clinically analytical in their thinking. This training doesn't leave much room for feeling. As Stephen explained when I asked him to write a piece for this book, "I do like writing, but I am so versed in conversing in the emotion-free world of the law that I have to feel my way when writing in different circumstances. It is quite hard getting the right blend of seriousness and lightness."

Believing that you can't do it puts up a barrier, of course. That was about to change dramatically. Here's Stephen's story.

Skulls in Action: What's in a Name?

I was lent a lapis skull by Judy to see how I got on with it. Immediately after I had been given it, which was at midnight at the College of Psychic Studies in South Kensington, I was walking down the stairs holding the skull in my left hand (I am right handed) and stopped to look at the long picture of the American medium Etta Wriedt over the lift. It seemed to be brightly lit. I looked at her face. Somehow it was hard to keep my focus and I started to see a number of faces each behind one another—moving in and out. I thought they were probably the same face but perhaps at different ages. All of a sudden, my whole aura filled up with very energetic fizzing gold light. It was extremely surprising; it was as though I were being "powered." After a period, I must have moved as the corridor light clicked on and the energy dissipated. I realised it had not been as light as I had thought.

Judy had said the skull would tell me his name. I assume she already knew he was male. I didn't expect him to but on the way to the underground, he definitely told me his name was Percy. I tried to get the name out of my mind as it seemed so unlikely. However, when I asked if he wanted a change of name (a sort of a legal joke), there was silence. Obliquely to quote Lewis Carroll "But answer came there none." I think in retrospect it is not a good idea to question some-body's name. However, I pondered the only other Percy that I knew—the name of the Norman knights (Perci) which of course became one of our oldest surnames. Then the names Percival/Perceval and then Parsifal (the opera) came to me. When I looked at the history of the story of Perceval and what it symbolises, it suddenly seemed an extremely powerful and purposeful name that I had not originally contemplated. It now seems entirely right.

Percy came in extremely useful last Saturday morning when I overslept by an hour and had to get to the College in South Kens-ington by 10:00 a.m. I woke at 9:05 a.m. in the Barbican in London and had only 55 minutes to get there including me showering/shav-ing etc. This seemed totally impossible—a distance of several miles across Central London. With his help however, we arrived at 9:45 a.m. precisely. On the journey, I held him in my left hand and as we approached traffic lights, I asked him to hold the green light as long as possible. He was successful most of the time. When we arrived, the taxi driver said "that was a very unusual journey." I thanked the skull profusely—hoping it was not an illegitimate use of him.

It didn't strike me as an illegitimate use of a skull's powers. We have to deal with the everyday while we're here, so why shouldn't they? Stephen is now clearly strongly connected to his skull, who communicates through Stephen's "inner knowing" perception mode:

I woke up at 4:00 a.m. the other morning and had to go up to the sitting room where he was and bring him down. I can't say exactly that he called me, but I just knew that was what I had to do. I put him by the bed.

Stephen didn't make the connection between his skull and a dream he then had. I did. Skulls so often work through sound.

I had a strange dream last night—someone was explaining something to me and they went into an entirely foreign dialect but it wasn't so much foreign more an entirely different way of communicating—it was noise but didn't sound even to have words exactly in the way we have them. It wasn't a white noise but it was a noise and even in the dream, I was surprised that I could even hear what it was as I knew I didn't understand what it meant. This sounds so bizarre now but I will see if the dream and what the content of the message was settles during the day.

Percy's sitting on the desk with me—and, I don't know if it is the light—but he is really laughing—at me possibly.

Stephen's new companion is another Arthurian-attuned skull. It is the grail knight who initially failed to ask the question that would have healed the wounded Fisher King, but who, in the end, came through. As did Stephen.

But that wasn't the end of Stephen's crystal skull experience. It expanded rapidly once the initial contact had been made, and his collection of skulls and other crystals grew apace. This is his most recent report:

After having acquired a rose quartz skull from Judy, which was particularly useful in dealing with a rather complex ancestral clearance case, I acquired a large orange calcite crystal skull which originated in Mexico. It has a thin but very noticeable white line diagonally through it which makes it look as though it has been struck by lightning. I brought it back to the College and on the way down Cromwell Road, I heard the name "Herbie." I was not thinking about names but after my experience with Percy/Perceval, I thought "Oh no, not another one with an unsuitable name." When I got to the College, Edwin Courtney was there and I showed him the skull and told him about its name. He said immediately (his response was so immediate I knew it was not the result of thinking): "You misheard. The name is Hebe—the goddess of fertility. [Hebe was the goddess of youth and the cupbearer to the gods. She served ambrosia at their feasts. She was also the patron goddess of young brides and an attendant of the goddess Aphrodite (Venus), goddess of love.] Orange calcite is very good for restoring mental and emotional equilibrium and for the uplifting energy it brings. This made perfect sense to me.

I took the skull to my flat and left it in its wrapping overnight. I got up quite early the next morning—a quiet Sunday—unwrapped it and put it on a shelf on the staircase next to a Tang horse, a Han dog, and a large Han amphora. The staircase is open plan so the skull can see both the downstairs and the front door and the upper floor. I brought the two small skulls to see it and suddenly the whole flat was abuzz. I thought at first that it was only the horse and the dog, but then I realized that everything was energised and communicating. A Tang camel in the kitchen which had been broken by the removal men reminded me it had been lying there broken for 18 months and that I had forgotten it. Clearly it wished to be mended. Then I was amazed to realise that the TV and the photocopier were also alive and reminding me of their presence. I was staggered. I realised that in fact the skull had energised absolutely every cell in the flat including the carpets and walls and, I supposed, me. I wandered around in a daze holding the two skulls and generally being amazed. Then I started to think about it and the whole effect subsided.

Someone said later that day that all the skull had done was awaken knowledge within me, but Judy said it was that but also that the skulls do indeed have the power to animate everything. So that was another amazing experience with skulls for me.

Should I Let Other People Handle My Crystal Skull?

That rather depends on the purpose of the skull and how you are working with it. A skull picks up energy from anyone who handles it. Most skullkeepers prefer to keep their skull clear of other people's energy unless it is actually performing healing or offering direct guidance. Some skull users, however, allow someone to handle the skull before giving a reading in the same way that a questioner is invited to shuffle tarot cards. It creates an immediate connection between the skull and the person seeking guidance or healing. If you are healing with your skull, you may feel it appropriate to place it on the recipient's body. If you do allow someone else to handle the skull, remember to cleanse the energies thoroughly afterward before you connect to the skull again yourself.

A Gentle Reminder: Cleanse Your Crystal Skull Regularly!

- As long as your skull is not friable, layered, or a many pointed or hollow geode, run the skull under water (spring or mineral water is preferable). Or, use a purpose-made cleansing essence (see Resources at the end of the book).

- Place the skull in the sunshine for several hours to recharge, or use a purpose-made essence.

- If the skull is delicate, place it in brown rice, smudge it, or place it on a cleansing crystal (see pages 96–97 for alternative cleansing methods).

Crystal Skulls in Action: The Watchers of Earth

The following is from Cas Lake, host of the radio show *The Unexplained Show* on *www.myspiritradio.com*.

It was late evening, about 11:00 p.m., and I remember lying in bed holding the crystal skull in both of my hands. I wanted to try and connect with the crystal skull before I went to sleep. It was nice to hold my crystal skull again after it had been on loan to another person. I cleansed the crystal skull first with Sekhem (a form of Reiki energy), and then tuned in quite quickly.

I started seeing images and feeling thoughts, it was like the crystal skull had an energy of its own and could communicate, but I don't know how it works. The skull suddenly showed me a printed newspaper that was black print and white, and then I felt the skull had been around someone with a newspaper and in a white building, it appeared to be like an old styled house. There was negative energy around, and I had a feeling in this building a policeman was popping in and wanted to buy the crystal skull. I felt the crystal skull had more of a male type energy and a feeling that the crystal skull's name started with an M, and then I got a feeling of what its name is.

Suddenly I was shown extreme heat to melting point, and I saw fire and then something melting, I soon realised this was what had happened to my crystal skull. I was next shown in my mind a stone-looking underground room. A bright natural looking light shone down from the ceiling to the floor. It reminded me of something I had read (I believe in the Emerald Tablets of Thoth, or the Book of Enoch) about the Watchers of Earth deep underground in our planet, and there was meant to be a light/fire of life.

I was soon informed by the crystal skull it was a baby (young in age for its kind). I presume it is a younger crystal; although it's designed like an alien's face, this crystal appears very much also connected to the Earth and the present. I admit I expected something linked with space when I first connected again with it, although I did feel two presences in my bedroom that I believe were entities of energy, but that was only for about a minute.

I thanked the crystal skull for what I was shown and felt, and then put it on the bedside cabinet beside me and dropped off to sleep.

CHAPTER 14

Physical, Psychic, and Earth Healing

Crystal skulls are versatile healers used either by direct contact or from a distance. In this context "healing" means bringing back into energetic balance rather than implying a cure. It improves well-being. The material from which a skull is carved heightens the effect (see the crystal directory at the end of the book). As with all things skull-related, there are several ways of accessing the energetic effect. Experimentation is needed until you identify the most efficient way for you. Some people find placing the skull directly on the body helpful. Skulls can also be placed at the head of a crystal layout to channel energy into the energetic net that this creates. Holding a skull or keeping contact with it either mentally or through the eyes is an effective method of channeling healing energy over vast distances.

Setting the Intention

Setting an intention directs energy appropriately. Holding your skull, ask it to assist with the healing you are about to undertake. Be specific. Define what the problem is and where the healing needs to go. This is particularly important if you are sending distant healing. Skulls do not always pay attention to what is going on in the everyday and may need focusing. Do not limit your skull, however. Ask that the healing be for the highest good of the person or place receiving it, and that anything else that is appropriate be offered at the same time. This is particularly important when there might be underlying causes of dis-ease, a state resulting from physical imbalances, blocked feelings, suppressed emotions, and toxic thinking that, if not reversed, leads to physical, psychiatric, or psychosomatic illness. Emotional or mental healing may also be required for what appears, on the surface, to be a physical problem but that actually has a deeper psychosomatic cause. The skull is aware of this need once focused.

Edwin Courtney's Skull Hold to Assist with Channeling the Skull's Energy

TOP OF CRANIUM HOLD
With the skull resting on your lap or a table, place both hands on top of the skull's cranium.

Physical Healing

Physical healing is carried out by placing the skull directly over the site of an injury, symptom, or pain. Or, hold the skull in your hands and direct a beam of healing to the site. The skull can also be positioned over your head and a layout in crystals placed over the chakras or around your body. Ensuring that your skull is energetically "full" assists the healing.

Charging Up a Crystal Skull to Give Healing

- Thoroughly cleanse the skull.
- Hold your skull up to the light of the sun, or use the power of your imagination.

- Picture the skull being filled with light and energy. Feel the potent life force that is activating the skull. Feel the loving, healing energy that is activated.

- State your intention.

Using Your Charged Crystal Skull for Yourself

- Hold your skull in your hands and feel the energy contained within it passing into your hands, up your arms, and through your chest into your heart. From your heart, the healing energy passes out to every part of your body, moving between and into your cells and the subtle layers of the biomagnetic sheath around your physical body. Allow the process. Do not force it. The process brings balance at the physical, emotional, mental, and spiritual level of being.

Using a Skull on the Chakras

The chakras are energetic portals linking your physical and subtle energetic bodies. Each chakra links to physical organs and various processes in the body. A chakra may feel dead, blocked, and closed. Or it may feel overactive, spinning wildly out of control. Chakra imbalances frequently lead to physical dis-ease and discomfort and a skull quickly brings the chakra back into balance.

- Placing your hand over the chakra or dowsing it quickly establishes if a chakra is spinning too fast or too slow.

- Place your skull over a chakra that is out of balance. Feel the energy equalizing and harmony returning to your body.

Chakras and Physiology

Earth star (below feet): physical body, electrical and meridian systems, sciatic nerve, and sensory organs.

Palms: nerves, tendons, ganglions, skin, hands, fingers, nails.

Knees: brain, kidneys, lumbar spine, heart, bladder and kidney meridians, sciatic nerve.

Base: fight-or-flight response, adrenals, bladder, elimination systems, gonads, immune system, kidneys, lower back, lower extremities, sciatic nerve, lymph system, prostate gland, rectum, skeletal system (teeth and bones), veins.

Sacral: bladder and gallbladder, immune and elimination systems, kidneys, large and small intestine, lumbar and pelvic region, sacrum, spleen, ovaries, testes, uterus.

Solar plexus: adrenals, digestive system, liver, lymphatic system, metabolism, muscles, pancreas, skin, small intestine, stomach, eyesight.

Heart: chest, circulation, heart, lungs, shoulders, thymus, respiratory system.

Higher heart (over thymus): psychic and physical immune systems, thymus gland, lymphatic system, elimination and purification organs.

Chakras and Physiology

Throat: ears, nose, respiratory and nervous system, sinuses, skin, throat, thyroid, parathyroid, tongue, tonsils, speech and body language, metabolism.

Third eye (brow): brain, ears, eyes, neurological and endocrine systems, pineal and pituitary glands, hypothalamus, production of serotonin and melatonin, temperature control, scalp, sinuses.

Crown: brain, central nervous system, hair, hypothalamus, pituitary gland, spine, subtle energy bodies, cerebellum, nervous motor control, posture and balance.

Past life (behind the ears): karmic blueprint and etheric bodies, psychosomatic dis-ease.

Alta major (inside the head): subtle and physical endocrine systems including the hippocampus, hypothalamus, pineal, and pituitary glands; brain function, cerebellum, voluntary muscle movements, medulla oblongata (controlling breathing, heart rate, and blood pressure); hormonal balance, occipital area and optic nerve, throat, spine, sleeping patterns.

Causal vortex (above and to one or other side of the head): etheric and karmic blueprint, inherited and karmic diseases, DNA and RNA.

(Extracted from *Crystal Prescriptions* volume 4.)

Skulls and Healing Layouts

Crystal skulls combine extremely well with crystal layouts. Crystal layouts are geometric shapes or "energy nets" created with crystals laid on or around your physical body. The crystals to use in the layout are best dowsed for in the same way that you select your skull (see pages 91–93). Bear in mind that certain crystals have specific healing properties. (The directory at the end of the book gives brief details. Also see my *Crystal Bibles*, *101 Power Crystals*, or *Crystal Prescriptions* for in-depth crystal profiles.)

BALANCING YOUR ENERGIES LAYOUT

Lie down for this layout. Ask a friend to assist if possible. If not, lay the crystals around your upper body, sit up and reach forward to lay the crystals around your lower body, and then lie down to place the crystals on your body. You can change the order of laying them out to what is convenient for you. It will not affect the energy flow.

- Place the skull above your head or on your chest, facing you if it feels more appropriate.

- Place pairs of crystals one either side of your head around the level of your ears.

- Place crystals at shoulder level.

- Place crystals level with your heart.

- Place crystals slightly above and below your waist.

- Place crystals at your knees.

- Place an earthing crystal such as Smoky Quartz, Flint, Black Tourmaline, or Hematite at your feet.

- Relax and close your eyes for ten to twenty minutes having asked the skull to direct healing and harmony as appropriate.

- When the healing is complete, gather up the crystals. Thank your skull. Stamp your feet to ground yourself or picture your grounding root going deep into the Earth (see page 112).

- Then cleanse the crystals and the skull.

Keeping your skull with you facilitates the energy balancing to go on working for you.

Psychic Healing

Psychic healing literally means "healing the psyche," rather than necessarily referring to metaphysical healing. There is, of course, an element of the latter as it is beyond the physical. Psychic healing works on the emotional, mental, and spiritual levels of being and on the subtle bioenergetic bodies that surround the physical—the aura. It is mediated by the chakras (the energy portals that link the physical and subtle bodies). The material from which the skull is made impacts the healing, so it is sensible to choose a skull that resonates on all levels with the healing required.

TO HEAL YOUR PSYCHE

- Place your skull either above your head or over your heart depending on where your intuition or the skull directs.

- Place an earthing crystal such as Smoky Quartz, Flint, Black Tourmaline, or Hematite at your feet.

- Other crystals can be placed over the chakras or around your body as appropriate.

- Relax and close your eyes for ten to twenty minutes having asked the skull to direct healing and harmony as appropriate. You may become aware of blockages, traumas, or beliefs being released. If so, direct them to the earthing crystal at your feet for transmutation and release.

- When the healing is complete, gather up the crystals, and thank your skull. Stamp your feet to ground yourself. Then cleanse the crystals and the skull.

Crystal Skull in Action: Sharing the Love

I had to leave my beloved marital home and temporarily move back in with my parents. My husband was a recovered heroin addict who had lived a challenging life on the streets before he'd found a way to turn his life around. We'd had a happy relationship for several years. But recently he'd started drinking heavily and was behaving like a misogynistic chauvinist. Staying out late, not helping with chores, and being exceedingly grumpy were the surface manifestations. But there was a deeper pain there. He had been adopted and had been estranged from his adoptive family for many years. He'd recently reconnected with them but had never traced his birth mother who, he felt, had abandoned him and he had no idea why. He was, however, unable to speak about this.

By his behavior, I felt he was abandoning me even though I'd been an enormous support to him. We seemingly worked things out on a holiday together and I moved back in.

Treating myself with a UV light for a skin condition, I fell asleep and suffered severe burns over my heart. Judy brought Rosebud, a very small Rose Quartz dragon skull to see me, explaining that the crystal not only helps to heal burns but is also excellent for the heart. The skull had a very gentle being connected to it. I immediately felt wrapped in love. Judy also brought me a new stone Ancestralite, which heals the ancestral line, and a rare Morganite with Azeztulite combination stone that encourages speaking the previously unspeakable. She said it had helped many of her clients access their suppressed feelings.

We worked with my heart chakra, which had been seriously scarred from a previous relationship. My work involves traumatized people, and Judy felt that I needed an interface, a kind of external protection around my aura, rather than the internal one I had created to shield my heart. Rosebud was full of unconditional love and poured this in to dissolve the scarring and heal the burn so that the chakra could expand and the interface be created. I felt deeply bathed in love. Within a day or two the burn, which had been deep and badly blistered, had healed. Rosebud had given healing to me at the physical and emotional level.

Afterwards I took Rosebud home and placed her by my bed. I hoped that in this way the energy would also assist my husband. The other two crystals were placed on either side. When he came in, surly and late again, I exploded in anger, letting out all my painful feelings. When I calmed down, we were able to talk in depth for the first time. To my amazement the next evening my husband began to speak to an acquaintance about the pain of being adopted. He had never done this before, even to close friends. I felt that something very profound had shifted for him. He was also able to directly express his frustration at the way his bandmates used him as an errand boy rather than treating him as a valued member of the band. He was no longer bottling up his feelings.

A week or two later we were at a music festival and he rushed over to tell me that he'd found a charity stall seeking sponsors for children in third world countries. Holding a pint of beer in his hand, he said that he'd realised that what he'd paid for it could provide a child with all that was needed for a week. So we sponsored a child together but decided that, rather than pick a "special" one out from a photograph, we would ask the charity to select an anonymous child for us. While we were organizing this, my husband shared his own story with the stallholder, a complete stranger. Rosebud had cracked open his heart and let in love and light. He was able to heal his damaged inner child by taking care of the needs of another child. Our relationship is blossoming under Rosebud's gentle guidance. And the skull has helped me to find words in challenging situations that would previously have been impossible for me to verbalize and handle with ease.

(Name withheld for confidentiality)

Healing Others

Crystal skulls and the layouts can also be used to heal other people. Simply place the layouts around them and ask the skulls to do their work. Dowse for appropriate crystals or ask the skulls to communicate what they wish you to use.

DISTANCE HEALING

As the skulls are not limited by the constraints of time, distance, and space, they send healing anywhere it is needed. Distance healing is best carried out when you can sit quietly with your skull for fifteen to twenty minutes. Hold the skull in your hands or have it on a table in front of you. Face it in toward you or out toward the person concerned. Place your hands on the skull if that feels appropriate.

- Bring the person to mind that is in need of healing. Hold a strong mental picture of them, or use an actual photograph if you have one.
- Ask your skull to send healing as appropriate to that person.
- Sit quietly with your skull until the healing is complete.
- Then let the picture fade and your connection dissolve.
- Thank your skull and cleanse it appropriately.

In an emergency, simply bring your skull to mind together with the person and ask that healing be sent as appropriate.

The same method is used to send healing, resolution, and peace to a distant situation or place. When appropriate, place your skull on a map or photograph and leave it in position.

Earth-Healing

As we have discovered, all skulls are connected to one another like a vast crystalline network: the Crystal Conclave. For those with the clairvoyant eyes to see it, Earth is also surrounded by a subtle energetic grid, its meridian lines joined in geometric shapes. The skulls have communicated that they are here to raise the vibrations of that grid, and the planet, so that more light is assimilated and the darkness of ignorance lifted.

Many indigenous skullkeepers report that the skulls have an important role to play in the activation of dormant energies within Earth's ley lines (meridian lines carrying earth energy). The skulls also assist with detoxifying and reharmonizing earth energies that have become stagnant or disturbed. Placed on the ground, they function rather like acupuncture needles, relieving blockages and encouraging the free flow of the planet's Qi (life force).

HEALING THE EARTH WITH YOUR CRYSTAL SKULL

This exercise is best carried out outdoors so that the skull is in sunlight placed in contact with the ground, be it grass, rock, soil, a beach, a desert, or in water. It is particularly appropriate at sacred sites or the crossing points of ley lines, or any site that has undergone trauma. You can also use the power of your imagination to connect to such a place, or position the skull on a map. Use one skull alone, or several in a circle or grid layout, and add in other crystals if this feels appropriate. Typical layout shapes are spiral, starburst (several lines radiating out from a central point that would be the skull), five-pointed star, or a Star of David (two overlapping triangles forming a six-pointed star). It does not matter how big or small the skulls and crystals are. Although the instructions are for the whole planet, you can also use this exercise to focus on just one area. Your skull and layout can be placed on a map if you wish to bring healing to a specific place.

- Place your skull at a central point.
- If you are using other skulls or crystals to form a layout, place these appropriately. Join up the shape with the power of your mind or a crystal wand.

- Breathe in deeply and feel your connection with the Earth and the life-giving sun. Bring to mind how your body is nurtured and nourished by the Earth. Feel the love and gratitude you have for the Earth. Let this love and gratitude flow into your skull and the layout. If it feels right, place your hand on the main skull while this energy is transmitted deep into the Earth. Be aware of the Earth receiving this love and being fertilized by the light of the sun.

- Maintain an even rhythm, breathing love, light, and gratitude into the planet.

- Feel or picture the sun above you, blazing its life-giving light down into your skull and your own cranium.

- Become aware of Earth's meridian grid. You may see it with your inner eye or sense it. Notice where it is broken or in need of healing.

- Then ask your skull to transmit healing light and transmutation to the Earth's grid so that it travels to every part. Be aware that the vibrations and frequency of the planet are being uplifted by this healing light.

- When the healing is complete, send love and peace to maintain the grid and reach all those who live on the planet.

- Thank your skull for its work and disconnect your energy as you gather up the layout.

- Cleanse your skull and any crystals used thoroughly.

Skulls in Action: Working with the Skulls for Earth-Healing by Alphedia Arara

I channel various crystal skull grid layouts for Earth healing. I also use knowledge Edwin Courtney brought through from his skulls, in particular the sacred Lemurian chant "Lem," to activate them. The skulls respond to this chant being repeated over and over. As a skull guardian you require to be grounded and be holding your awareness in your heart centre, thus allowing the highest healing possible while chanting. The skulls contain energetic blueprint templates. They are able to overlay these templates to bring an area back into balance. Ask the skulls to correct any earth energy anomalies and to bring the area you are working on back into harmony. You may feel the Earth shake beneath your feet at this point, depending on how much correction is required. After you feel this is complete, you can ask the skulls to overlay an etheric temple of light or the new divine blueprint Gaia, Mother Earth, wishes to be held in this area. You can also ask your skulls to collect any wisdom or Earth codes that would be of benefit for the skull's work on Earth and your own. You can do this work with just one skull, however I have found it is more powerful with lots of skulls being present and with their guardians also holding the space and working intuitively. At each site the skulls have been asked to be laid out differently so go with intuition. After the healing you will feel the land energy has changed, you may see visions or symbols as you do the activation. Skulls also see no physical barriers to their work and will ask to be taken up mountains, out on boats, and often to locations where one has to walk miles through peat bogs! By clearing the land energy this allows it to increase in vibration allowing the people who live on it or connect with it to increase in consciousness even if sub-consciously. I believe the skulls are reconnecting webs of light with this work. I hold a free crystal skull earth healing gathering each year in an area I am guided to perform an activation on.[1]

Crystal Skulls in Action: Healing the Earth, Knowlton Henge, Summer Solstice 2015

As soon as my Smoky Quartz skull Horace had revealed his name, his earth-healing powers blossomed. I had a collection of Celtic Golden Healer Quartz that I had gathered on a trip to Wales. It had told me that it wanted to go around the world to form a healing grid to bring harmony to a benighted planet. But it needed activating first. So, Horace, Gawain (my Preseli Blue-stone), the Celtic Quartz, and my fellow astrologer and earth-worker Terrie Birch and I went to Knowlton Henge, my local sacred site, to celebrate the summer solstice. We laid out a vast spiral of the Quartz on a zodiac wheel, aligned to the four direc-tions and several local ley lines. Horace, Gawain, and Terrie's clear Quartz skull anchored the corners with the fourth open for the energy to travel into Earth's grid. As we laid the last crystal, the sun burst out from behind the clouds. Horace came alive as the solar light pierced his eyes and cranium. Golden rainbows flared within him. They flashed into a huge Welsh Calcite at the core and ignited the gleaming spiral. It was a truly magical moment as light blazed into the land.

The author and the 2015 summer solstice crystal layout at Knowlton Henge
(Terrie Birch/www.astrologywise.co.uk)

Crystal Skulls

At that moment, two guys who had been circling the henge stopped alongside where I stood on the bank, facing west. It was late in the day and we were honoring the astrological solstice and the moment the sun changed signs. They saluted and thanked the sun for its light, before murmuring "beautiful, thankful" to the layout below which by now was incandescent with light. They moved on to honor the remaining directions as the sun slowly fell toward its midsummer setting point. We gathered up our crystal friends and gave thanks for the healing that had taken place just as the sun disappeared and the rain clouds moved in to thoroughly cleanse the land.

Healing the Ancestral Line

All too often dis-eases pass down through the ancestral line—the family trees on each side of your parentage that go back way into the past and out into future generations. These dis-eases may be conveyed genetically or through attitudes and toxic belief systems handed on from generation to generation. There is no need for you to know the details to feel the results. Crystal skulls are partic-ularly efficient at healing the ancestral line and sending the heal-ing forward across time so that future generations are released.

- Ask your skull to assist you in healing your ancestral line.
- Face your skull forward.
- Place your hands on the skull's cranium. Your fingers nat-urally go to the back of the cranium.
- Close your eyes and breathe gently.
- Become aware of the ancestral line unrolling behind you like the roots of a tree going way back into the past with branches going forward into the future.
- Ask the skull to send healing back down the line to release all the blockages, traumas, dramas, and toxic thoughts and emotions that scar the line.

- If the dis-ease is passed on genetically, ask the skull to switch off the negative potential of your genes and to switch on "good vibes." Feel the healing settling into the spaces between your cells and passing into the cell walls, adjusting your DNA as it goes.

- When the healing is complete and the energy has returned to the present, request the skull to send healing and gifts out into the future for the generations to come so that the positive aspect of the ancestral line is manifested.

- Disconnect and thank the skull for its assistance.

- Cleanse your skull thoroughly.

CHAPTER 15

Scrying with Your Crystal Skull

Crystal skulls can be used to channel personal insights, or to give guidance readings for other people. Or to scry: that is, to see the past, present, or future in the crystal. Channeling with a skull assists the wise beings to share galactic knowledge of what is to come and reveal how humanity can best cooperate with the energetic shifts now taking place. Some skulls prefer to work in an intimate, one-on-one fashion. Others want to spread their word through addressing large groups of people or putting out messages on the Internet.

The holds below are the ones I and my crystal groups have found to be helpful. Edwin Courtney's specific channeling and activation holds (see below) also assist you to channel your skull. Try different holds and methods until you find the one best suited to your way of receiving and conveying information. Once you have had practice, you'll find that putting out the thought that you wish to communicate is sufficient to begin the process.

Scrying or Channeling for Yourself

Once you have attuned to your skull (see page 99) and established whether you find it easier to look into or out from your skull's eyes, or whether you actually *hear* your skull or *sense* what is being said to you, pose specific questions or ask for guidance or information that is of benefit either in your everyday or spiritual life.

TO SEE YOUR CRYSTAL SKULL'S MESSAGE

- Place your fingers at the corner of your skull's eyes or over its third eye. Or, following the information on holds below, gaze into the cranium, into or out through its eyes. Images are stimulated by first holding your skull's third eye to your third eye.

- Alternatively, place your fingers as above and gaze into the skull's cranium if it is a clear rather than opaque crystal.

TO HEAR YOUR CRYSTAL SKULL'S MESSAGE

- Hold your skull slightly behind your dominant ear, the one you turn forward in order to hear better, with the lips close to your ear.

TO INTUIT OR SENSE YOUR CRYSTAL SKULL'S MESSAGE

- Place your hands over the skull's cranium with your fingers on the skull's third eye if it is facing toward you, or place the thumbs along the base and your fingers over the skull's third eye if facing out.

- Or, place your skull's third eye to your own third eye. Leave it there or position the skull in your lap or on a table in front of you.

EDWIN COURTNEY'S SKULL HOLDS
FOR CHANNELING AND CLAIRVOYANCE

To see with the skulls (clairvoyance): the eye socket hold

With the skull on your lap or resting on a table and facing away from you, place the fingers of both hands into each of the skull's eye sockets.

Third eye hold

With the skull resting in your lap or on a table, rest both hands on the top of the cranium and reach forward to rest the first two fingers of both hands on the third eye (brow center) of the skull.

Note: you may need to try this hold with the skull facing toward and then away from you to find the one that is most effective for you.

To assist with processing spiritual information:
the base of cranium hold
With the skull on your lap or table facing toward you, place one hand on the base of the cranium at the back and the other on top of it.

Skulls in Action: Establishing a Connection
Although outwardly tall and physically robust, Joe was a sensitive guy with largely untapped intuitive abilities. He cheerfully volunteered to try out communicating with a skull even though, he admitted later, he had little expectation of getting a result. Joe had just undergone a traumatic relationship breakup and was unsure of the direction he needed to take in life. The skull he chose was a large, clear Quartz with many inclusions and inner planes. In attuning to the skull, he used a number of psychic perception modes, including the visual and aural, but his primary focus was sensing. However, it wasn't until he made his report to me afterward that it became clear to him exactly how the skull had been communicating. All part of the learning process!

A Case of the Rumbles
I first looked into the skull's eyes—it was on a table facing me. I placed my hands either side of the cranium and instinctively bent my head and touched my third eye (located on the forehead above and between the eyebrows) to that of the skull. I could feel an instant connection. Lifting my head, I gazed into the skull's cranium. I sat entranced for several minutes. It was as though the eyes were holding

me in a beam of light. At the skull's prompting, I closed my eyes and withdrew my attention from the outside world.

After ten minutes of sitting quietly with my hands still on the skull I was able to speak of what had been happening, which clarified things for me. I had initially seen the inside of the skull rapidly pulsating and whirling rather like a cyclone. It was extremely disorienting. I quickly became aware that my belly was rumbling and roiling in exactly the same way. My solar plexus and sacral chakras felt very disturbed, and I instinctively knew this reflected my emotional distress, which I'd been trying to keep suppressed. Slowly both the skull and my gut gradually settled into quietness. My chakras became calm. When I closed my eyes, I was overwhelmed by a sense that all would be well. The skull was reassuring me. It was as though it picked me up and put me on the right path, I could feel myself shifting. It clearly said, "All is well."

Soon afterwards I was offered the job of my dreams. Not so long after that, I began a new relationship.

Scrying or Channeling for Others

Individual scrying or channeling sessions for others are a great way to expand your crystal skull attunement. When scrying, you see pictures or hear information that you relay without interpretation. The pictures may be of past, present, or future. If the information is not clear, ask for further clarification.

- If it feels appropriate, allow the sitter to hold the skull to make a connection for a few moments before you begin to scry or to channel.

- Hold the skull in your lap facing out toward the sitter so that you see through the skull's eyes, or gaze into the skull's cranium.

- The sitter can ask a direct question or be open to what the skull has to say.

- Wait until the information drops into your head and

then pass it on. Or, if you have learned to trust your skull implicitly, open your mouth and start to speak. Trust that the skull has something to say even though you do not know what it is until it comes out of your mouth. People often surprise themselves with the result. If the channeling makes no sense, do not be afraid to end it and wait until another time.

- When the scrying or channeling is complete, disconnect your attention from the skull and the other person. Covering the skull with a cloth is often sufficient. When the other person leaves, closing the door on them cuts the energetic tie if this has not been completely cleared at the end of the session.

You do not need the other person to be physically present to channel skull guidance. You can speak by phone or Skype, or write down or record the message as you receive it.

Channeling for the Collective

If you are channeling for the collective, you may need a scribe or recorder unless you are able to write or type at speed. Channeling for the collective most often takes place in front of a group, but it may also be a transcription for Internet dissemination. Channeling in front of a large group is best done after you have regularly practiced in a small development group first to ensure that the quality and flow of your channeling is of the highest.

- Hold your skull in the way that you find most effective (see pages 128–129 and 144–145), or place it on a table alongside you if you have established a strong rapport.
- Follow the directions above.

How to Work with Your Crystal Skull   147

CHAPTER 16

Reading the Akashic Record

The Akashic Record is an ongoing record of the journey of the soul, and the long evolution of this and other worlds. A plane of pure potentiality, it could be called the cosmic memory field, although it is not bound by linear time. It can be viewed as a hologram or vast library of all that is, has been, and may be. Fortunately, you don't have to understand how the field exists nor how it works in order to be able to utilize it for insight into why you are here, where you've been, and where you are going.

The Akashic Record is a not a record of a fixed fate. Rather, it is an outline map of a soul's journey with all the potentialities that open up and the multidimensional realities in which your soul exists. This can, initially, be mind-boggling. It extends way out into the future with myriad possibilities to unfold as well as accessing the past and parallel lives—*all of which are happening at once.* Successful reading of the Akashic Record takes practice. Looking through the eyes of your skull speeds up the process.

If you are reading for someone else, always ask permission to be shown their Record, and only do so if they have agreed beforehand.

- Place your skull facing outward in front of you.
- Cup your hands around the skull with the thumbs along the ridge at the base and your index fingertips over the

third eye at the center of the forehead. Rest your other fingertips at the outer edge of the eye sockets.

- Ask your skull to access the Akashic Record and to show you your own personal record (or that of the other person).

- Gaze into the cranium of your skull and down into its eyes. Slightly narrow your eyes and let them go out of focus, or close them altogether if this is more comfortable for you and you have established that you see with your inner eye.

- Ask your skull to show you the portion of your Record that is appropriate for you now (or for the other person). If you have a specific question to which you need an answer, or a situation you need to understand, put that to your skull and ask to read the relevant section of the Record. Be prepared for that portion to be a past life or an ancestral theme.

- If the past needs healing or reframing, ask your skull to connect you to a timeline that brings resolution. The skull consciousness knows what is needed.

- The skull may show you several possibilities for the future. Ask to know which is the most appropriate for you and to be shown what you need to put in place in the present moment to ensure that you follow the most fitting path forward. You can seek guidance as to a right decision in this way. You can also seed tools and directions into the future to pick up when appropriate.

- When you have finished, thank your skull and disconnect your attention by taking your hands away.

CHAPTER 17

Journeying with Your Crystal Skull

Journeying with a skull means that your consciousness is transported away from your physical body. These days, rather than being regarded as an anomalous figment of the imagination, such journeys are designated Exceptional Human Experiences. They are recognized as life-changing, enriching, and worthy of study (see the research in my *Book of Psychic Development*). Journeys can be undertaken for healing, teaching, or exploration purposes. The journey may be a shamanic one to the lower, middle, or upper worlds, or one that takes you into another dimension entirely, as we will see.

The Neurochemical Looking Glass

Shamans over eons of time have journeyed to other realms. Under stimuli such as drumming, chanting, incantations, and magical brews, indigenous and psychically attuned people have long demonstrated the ability to journey out of their body. There are people who require no external stimulus at all, and others who find that a skull assists such journeys. If you are wondering how your consciousness can go walkabout, it seems to be a natural function of a human being. It could well be that small amounts of an endogenous neurochemical, dimethyltryptamine (DMT), in the brain are what facilitate your consciousness traveling and returning. Leading-edge researchers in the field of neurobiology have found that, during near-death experiences and out-of-body experiences such as shamanic journeying, DMT is synthesized in the brain. DMT has been dubbed the "Spirit molecule." The pineal gland, which secretes DMT, contains natural crystalline fluorapatite, "brain sand." It has long been metaphysically associated with the third eye and psychic experiences. It may be that the natural crystals in the pineal resonate with the vibrations from the skulls to stimulate DMT and the ability to go traveling.

To Journey with Your Crystal Skull

Journeying is best carried out lying down or comfortably relaxed in a chair. A shamanic drumming music track is helpful.

- Hold your skull in whichever hold you have established gives you the easiest access to information. Or place it above your head if you are lying down.

- Ask your skull to take you on a journey. If you have a specific destination or purpose in mind, state it. Or, ask your skull to take you wherever is most appropriate at this time.

- Close your eyes. Breathe gently and easily, allowing the skull to transport you and noting any images or feelings that arise.

- Once the journey is over, ask the skull to return you to your starting point.

- When you have returned, disconnect from your skull and thank it for the journey.

- Stand up and stamp your feet on the floor to reground yourself.

- Make a note of what you experienced.

Skulls in Action: Journeying with Horus

I was lovingly gifted a beautiful, large Amethyst skull. Somehow, the skull and I never really connected. It felt like I was only a temporary keeper. So I was delighted when, the first time my crystal group worked with my collection of skulls, that particular skull ended up in the lap of Emma Penman. They had clearly made a strong heart connection. Emma is a fantastic healer and body and energy worker with very profound crystal knowledge, so I knew that in her care the skull would be put to work immediately. She was one of the first to volunteer her experience with Horus, as he has intimated he is called, for this book:

With Horus out into the Cosmos

I asked my Amethyst skull Horus to guide me, he wanted to be face forwards sat on my lap. It soon became clear that he was taking me off on a journey. I was looking out from his eyes. We went straight out beyond this galaxy, surrounded by stars and out into the Cosmos. We connected with another star system and the beings inhabiting this space. I then soon realised that I was connecting with a multi-dimensional part of me that was based there. This reconnection was important to help me fulfill more of my soul purpose for this incarnation. The energy was beautiful, healing and it was exciting to experience this level of myself. Horus was showing me how I can easily connect with these other aspects of myself and teaching me this technique of working with him. It was wonderful.

The next day I received another email report from Emma:

I thought I would revisit yesterday's journey to get more information for you but Horus had a different idea so I asked him to guide me to wherever I needed to go for the greatest good, also calling in my team of helpers (my higher self, source, guides) to assist. We went straight down into the Earth, deeper and deeper down to the central crystal at the heart of Gaia. From this point we then connected out into the Earth's grid. I felt Gaia's energy connect in with me. So bright and loving, my body tingling and feeling like it was getting brighter and brighter. Energies started pouring through me from my higher connections, filling myself and the Earth. I felt like Horus and I were merged. All I could see was bright white, the energies so high that I could barely think. It felt wonderful, I could feel the energy spreading from the central crystal out into the Earth via the grids, filling it with this beautiful light. We eventually came up to the surface. I saw views of meadows and trees and was aware that it was being sent to help all life. It then spread out into the atmosphere. The light then started to dim and I felt my energy had returned to my body, I had a huge smile stuck on my face from the ecstatic feeling of the energy. A beautiful and powerful experience.

Crystal Skull in Action: Journeying to Creation

Animal or bird skulls may sometimes be more effective for shamanic journeying than humanoid ones. Here is my own experience of journeying with Raven, an Astrophyllite bird skull. As the name suggests, Astrophyllite has powerful cosmic connections. The crystal helps you to move forward in your life, infusing you with inner light. This wasn't why I'd bought the skull. It had reached out and seduced me with its hypnotic eyes when I was searching for something else entirely. Who could resist?

Soul Retrieval for the Earth

A blackish raven skull had called to me when I was trawling through the Skullis website. On closer inspection, I could see that the crystal was iridescent with shining streaks of gold and silver. It looked like a meteor shower falling through the night sky. It arrived just as I was about to lead a crystal medicine wheel workshop, so I took it along to represent air and put it beside a rather special raven's feather. Ravens nest just up the road from my home, and the previous year I had had the incredible experience of chatting to a young raven as it sat on a branch high above me. These birds really do talk! Having given me the soul guidance I needed, he'd dropped me the feather as we said goodbye.

Crinoid fossil Raven head
(www.skullis.com)

At the workshop, we turned toward the north and the element of air. We held Lemurian Seed crystals. A large one was placed on the wheel laid out in the center of our circle. I was sitting in the north and so was facing Raven. The skull's eyes gripped me as though they would never let me go. He linked me to the Lemurian crystal beside him and the one in my hand, moving me outside time. I was fully aware of leading the journey, guiding the group, and holding their space. At another level, I was immediately back in a shamanic journey I had undertaken a few years earlier under the guidance of a very skilled shaman drummer.

I was at the creation of our present universe. Clearly there had been something before, but what that was hadn't been clear in the original journey. Nor was it now (I promised myself I'd go back one day and find out). All I was aware of was an almighty explosion and an atomic bomb cloud of cosmic dust billowing out. Watchers, of which I was one, stood all around. Our job was to guide the process of recreation.

I found myself journeying in a cloud of dust, with large particles of gold and diamonds floating all around me. It was like being in a giant Astrophyllite crystal. I became aware that I was traveling alongside the Earth Mother. "I'm not from there either," she said conversationally and sighed deeply. I know exactly how she felt!

Slowly the dust cloud condensed and became compacted, wrapping itself around her. She was formed from dancing light, and the dust was smothering the life out of her as the heavy particles penetrated her energy body. I realized that her soul, her activating principle, had remained alongside me, watching in horror. So I took her soul by the hand and reconnected them as the particles swirled and came into form around a giant Hematite crystal that had also traveled with us. She was able to infuse the dense matter with her light, creating a meridian energy net to sustain her. I promised her that I would return to bring her fertilizing light whenever I could. I now do this regularly with my groups by visualizing taking Fire and Ice Quartz carrying the energy of the sun to her heart.

That's where the original journey had ended. I had been called back to my body, which I took over again reluctantly, having experienced the weightless bliss of my pure essence. Realizing that I needed to incorporate this essence into my self as I now am, in the form I have taken on, I have revisited the journey several times since then. It's why I'm so insistent when I work with groups that we ground the high vibrational energy, bringing it "down here" to where we live, literally en-lightening our physical bodies as well as our spiritual selves with the raised vibrations.

This time, however, Raven stepped in front of me. "This is your soul path," he said. "Expanding consciousness, helping people to know they are so much more than a physical body and returning crystal light into the Earth. Helping them to heal the Earth is so important. Write about it."

When I opened my eyes, Raven was pinning me with his gaze. His eyes were hypnotic. "Help me," I pleaded, "I have the structure for the book and most of the words. I just need a publisher."

"So be it," he replied. The seed for my book *Earth Blessings* had been activated. A week later it was accepted by a publisher. Thank you Watkins Publishing for cooperating so well with my Raven friend.

CHAPTER 18

Power Animal and Mythical Crystal Skulls

Crystal skulls are not necessarily humanoid or alien or star being in form. Some take on the characteristics of mythical beings such as the unicorn and power animals or birds. They are crystal allies that offer shamanic wisdom. Power animals are particularly useful for ancestral healing work and for accompanying shamanic journeys, providing protection and guidance. Power animal skulls are attuned to and worked with in exactly the same way as other skulls.

Dragon

A powerful representation of transmutation and change, and carriers of timeless wisdom, dragons embody auspicious powers, although these differ in eastern and western symbolism. Despite the hostile legends that have attached to them, they are guardian beings. With the exception of the cosmic dragons, dragons tend to have an earthier perspective than the humanoid skulls. The cosmic dragons are, however, moving closer to Earth once more and anchoring their consciousness in the skulls.

Skullkeeper Jeni Powell received this teaching from the dragon goddess Sofia via her own crystal dragon skulls:

Sofia states that the dragons are part of Earth's make-up to harmonise our planet's energies in line with external changes. All matter, including dragons, is comprised of minute energy particles and it is our mind that creates the image we wish to see. Hence the ley lines surrounding Earth (or dragon lines as they were once called) appearing to some as winged dragon creatures.

She has allowed me to work with and understand the Dragon community—learning about the different types of 'dragons' that are present on/in and around the Earth and also the crystal dragon energies (which are of a finer frequency and work in different dimensions). All of the dragons have a part to play in balancing Earth's energies and keeping our planet safe. To balance the planet it is now imperative to balance all that reside on her—including us. This is where the dragon energies come into play—we can work with them to harmonise our own energy systems so that we feel more positive, health,y and harmonious which has a knock on effect on mother earth. To this effect, Sofia has also instigated the creation of the Crystal Balance Dragon energy sprays which allow us to experience the different dragons and their qualities, helping us to feel at our optimum and completely balanced.

THE ELEMENTAL DRAGONS

In the western view, the elemental dragons represent the four directions and the five elements, as do different colors of dragon.

- **The creative fire dragon** of the East symbolizes energy, transmutation, and mastery of power. As with the colors red and orange, a fire dragon imbues you with vitality and enthusiasm, lending you the courage to overcome obstacles.

- **The nurturing earth dragon** of the West symbolizes your riches and your potential, inner and outer. As with the green, gray, brown, and speckled crystals, earth dragons are helpful when you need grounding and stabilizing.

Crystal Skulls

They pull together scattered energies and reintegrate them when you need to call on your deepest resources.

- **The inspirational air dragon** of the North offers you insight and illumination. Call on it when you need clarity or to connect to your intuition and inner guidance. Pale color crystals such as yellow, blue, and silvery-gray connect to its wisdom.

- **The empathetic water dragon** of the South offers you a deeper connection—to your own past and to ancestral memories. It links to your suppressed emotions and to the hidden desires that motivate you. Compassionate blue and blue-green as well as translucent crystals quickly access the water dragon and help you to come to terms with, and release, the past.

- **The assertive metal dragons** facilitate the flow around and within the planet of the energizing properties of metallic elements, especially those bound up within crystal beds. These dragons regulate the passage of life force within the Earth's meridians and can be called on to assist with earth-healing. Metal dragon skulls formed from Iron Pyrite, Hematite, and so on carry the same qualities. Their steely resolve is helpful if you need to stand up for yourself or take on a challenge.

According to Alphedia Arara, the metal dragons also work with metals that have been smelted and used in constructions and for flight. One of her dragons communicated:

Now that humanity has evolved to create massive metal structures on top of Gaia's skin, some of us are dwelling in the Earth's atmosphere as guardians of these great metallic structures. Some skyscrapers and buildings we are guardians of, and each aeroplane has a guardian dragon due to the high aluminium content and other metals used to transport people around the globe.

Their stated purpose is to create a greater connection with the metallic kingdom and speed up humanity's spiritual development. Isn't that a comforting idea, each plane in the sky having a dragon looking after it? It makes me look forward to my next flight.

Since I have begun writing this book, I have been reminded that there is another element: wood. I was on a crystal mountain in Wales, which has a huge golden dragon guardian, from which we collect dragon-shaped rocks and healing-infused crystals that go around the world to perform earth-healing. This mountain is literally created from the powerful Celtic Golden Healer Quartz, with white Celtic Chevron, Blue and Red Quartz within its granite matrix. Added to that are several minerals including lead, gold, and silver and the occasional Calcite. You never quite know what you'll uncover there. It is indeed a dragon's treasure trove. The site of a former lead mine, it has the most extraordinary energy. The mountain was planted with nonnative conifer trees when the mine closed, and these trees are now being harvested, which reveals many crystal beauties. But when a friend and I went to do some water-healing a few miles away where a dam had been created and a village drowned, we found that ancient native trees were being torn out to create parking places. Huge craters scarred the beautiful landscape, dead wood and displaced roots were all around. Torrential rain was stirring up the mud. The area was crying out for healing. I realized that, in our elemental healing ceremonies, we'd been neglecting the very important wood element that connects us to Nature and her cycles and seasons. That night

The author's Petrified Wood dragon (*www.skullis.com*)

I went online to buy the most gorgeous pink and gray striped Petrified Wood dragon.

- In Chinese five element acupuncture, wood represents the spring, the seeds of life, and the start of something new. Sociable Wood holds the ability to survive and has the strength to overcome obstacles. But unlike enduring stone, wood breaks down—and can be recycled. The renewing wood dragons first destroy all that is outworn and outgrown, and then usher in a new cycle. They are the endless pattern of growth and rebirth, decay and regeneration. But the flexible wood dragons offer us something more. Like the trees themselves, they have their roots deep in the ground and their leaves in the ether. They take in nourishment from the Earth and from the cosmos, combining the two into intrinsic balance. The wood dragons enable us to ground new awareness and anchor high vibrational energies deep into the Earth. With a wood dragon at our side, we can manifest all that we truly are. Petrified Wood, Peanut Wood, Amber, and similar stones access the wood dragons.

- The cosmic dragons are vast interstellar beings, wise beyond the range of human perception. Mythical and mystical, these dragons have been represented throughout time, but remained in other dimensions. These dragons are now drawing closer to Earth to share their wisdom and assist with human evolution. Natural dragon-shaped high-vibration crystals such as Celtic Quartz or Anandalite™, or Astrophyllite, or meteorite-infused stones such as Libyan Gold Tektite or Moldavite connect you to the cosmic dragons.

Condor

A symbol of timeless power and the natural cycle of birth, death, and rebirth, the independent condor soars effortlessly above the world to offer an objective, overall perspective on life. This is a useful skull when you need to understand the point of view of another person and harmonize it with your own. Connect to a condor skull if you wish to find your soul purpose and your inner vision. Fly with it to achieve your highest vision and wildest dreams.

Jaguar and Panther

Powerfully protective figures, jaguar or panther skulls represent strength, agility, and confidence. This power animal assists you to focus and call in your mystical powers. It guides you into the pathways that lead through chaos, showing you how to move fearlessly through necessary change. Panther is a natural shapeshifter and confers invisibility when traversing the other worlds. Use a jaguar skull to undertake a vision quest to your future.

Owl

Long regarded as a symbol of wisdom and discernment, owl offers you an all-around view. With its keen observation and binocular vision, it brings the distant close to you. This is a useful skull for opening the inner ear, whispering to you in the silence of meditation. With your owl skull's assistance, you gain clarity in the darkness of night. In ancient times, the owl was the guardian of the dead and assisted communication with the departed.

Raven

A profoundly mystical and magical bird, ravens help you to put aside fear and journey deep into the heart of the mysteries. With sharp intelligence, raven skulls assist you to solve the puzzles and conundrums in your life. It is a helpful skull to have with you if you want to write. According to psychologist Carl Jung, ravens represent the dark side of the self. This bird offers you a penetrating understanding of your inner self and how it creates the world you perceive around you. The raven's curiosity is legendary. According to the bible, it was the first bird sent out by

Noah (Genesis 8:7). It flew backward and forward until it was "sent forth and did not return." Where it landed, no one knew. In ancient times, the raven was an oracle bird. He was also a scavenger, searching through the dead and discarded to sustain himself. With a raven skull you move fearlessly through the unknown or the darker reaches of the psyche, seek out the riches secreted there, and penetrate the future or connect with the ancestors.

Ravens have a historic link with skulls, too, through the Welsh hero Bran the Blessed, whose name means "raven." Bran was the holder of ancestral memories, and his wisdom was legendary.

Tiger

A tiger skull strengthens your willpower and helps you to be independent. This is the perfect skull if you need to stand on your own two feet. The tiger represents the challenge to trust yourself and your primal instincts. The skull helps you deal with life spontaneously and joyfully, responding rapidly to challenges and changes. It endows you with the strength to overcome obstacles on the path to success.

Unicorn

Unicorn skulls are rare things. Magical creatures, unicorns tend to appear when there are secrets to be told and dreams to be made manifest. They have long been seen as symbols of magic, miracles, purity, innocence, and enchantment. Shape-shifters who flit effortlessly through multidimensions and endless cycles of time, unicorns occupy liminal spaces, those places at the edge of consciousness where profound Earth knowledge lies, but which also connect to the stars. Alphedia Arara received this channeled message from the unicorns: "[We are] offering to assist you in being able to step out of drama and to step back from fiery situations, allowing you smooth passage through turbulent energies. . . . The Unicorns are going to offer to open up a portal within you to assist you in being able to harness higher frequency light that is descending onto the planet." According to the Elemental Beings website (*www.elementalbeings.co.uk*), unicorns also "bring balance into your core central matrix . . . and show you the areas of your life [where] you are over expending energy and the areas of your life where you are under focusing."

Wolf

Wolf is a sociable clan animal, and this skull helps you to discern how you fit into the wider family, your place in society, and the impact you make. It assists in accessing the wisdom of your ancestors and exploring your roots. This skull teaches you who your true friends are. It also lends you the cunning of a wolf, as well as the ability to strategize and actualize your future. With a wolf you forge a new pathway, and then return to share it with your clan.

CHAPTER 19

Crystal Directory

When you are looking for a skull, you have many options, not only in shape but also in the material from which skulls are carved. Different types of crystal have varying properties, so you need to identify one that calls to you, fulfills your needs, and harmonizes with your purpose.

The Quartzes

Amethyst: Amethyst is the perfect dwelling for a spiritual mentor. Protective and potent, Amethyst calms the mind and makes you more receptive to information from expanded realities. It is attuned to the third eye and crown chakras.

Vibration: High to exceedingly high according to type. Also grounds the energy.

Healing qualities: Tunes the endocrine system and metabolism; strengthens eliminating organs and the immune system; relieves physical, emotional, and psychological pain or stress; treats insomnia. Amethyst balances the physical, mental, and emotional bodies, linking them to the spiritual.

Citrine: Citrine skulls tend to be occupied by wisdom keepers. This is a creative manifestation and regeneration crystal that realigns the subtle energy bodies and facilitates downloads of new information.

Vibration: High.

Healing qualities: Citrine is an eliminator, energizing and recharging. It activates the thymus and balances the thyroid. It has a warming effect and fortifies the nerves.

Clear Quartz: Quartz is highly energetic and retains a program or information download over long periods of time. This is a master healing crystal that aligns all the chakras and opens the higher crown.

Vibration: High to exceedingly high according to type. Also grounds the energy for healing.

Healing qualities: A master healer, Quartz is used for any condition. It stimulates the immune system and brings the body into balance, harmonizing the chakras and aligning the subtle bodies.

Rose Quartz: A stone of unconditional love and understanding, Rose Quartz is the perfect home for a healing guide. It is attuned to the three-chambered heart chakra and the soul.

Vibration: High. Also grounds the energy.

Healing qualities: Emotionally, Rose Quartz is the finest healer. Releasing unexpressed emotions and heartache, it transmutes emotional conditioning that no longer serves, soothing internalized pain and healing a sense of deprivation.

Smoky Quartz: Smoky Quartz assists with transitions, transmutations, and transformations. It facilitates letting go of whatever no longer serves and removes toxicity. The perfect skull for earth-healing, it is attuned to the base chakra and the earth star (beneath the feet).

Vibration: Earthy and high according to type. It grounds and transmutes energy for healing.

Healing qualities: An excellent detoxifying crystal, tolerance of stress is much improved with the assistance of relaxing Smoky Quartz. This stone provides pain relief.

Higher vibrational Quartzes such as **Lemurian Seed** are attuned to the chakras above the head and have less effect on the physical body. They are excellent for hosting interdimensional beings.

Note: Skulls are also available in reconstituted Quartz. Reputable sellers inform you that this is the case.

Other Crystals

Agate: Agates have very stable energy that balances and harmonizes. The stone facilitates acceptance of oneself and others without judgment. The color and type subtly affects the properties of the skull and the chakra with which it resonates.

Vibration: Earthy.

Healing qualities: Agate stabilizes the aura. Its cleansing effect is powerful physically and emotionally. It heals emotional dis-ease that prevents acceptance of love.

Amazonite: A stone with exceptional filtering qualities and the power to soothe the nervous system, this stone maintains optimum health by balancing the physical and subtle energy bodies.

Vibration: Earthy.

Healing Qualities: Amazonite opens the heart and throat chakras. It also opens the third eye and the intuition. The stone dissipates negative energy and blocks within the nervous system.

Astrophyllite: A stone that reaches the stars and accesses the limitless potential of your soul. Activating "dreaming true" to see your soul path, Astrophyllite promotes out-of-body experiences and acts as guide and protector in other realms. It is the perfect receptacle for a star being mentor.

Vibration: High.

Healing Qualities: Astrophyllite assists the hormonal and nervous systems and cellular regeneration.

Atlantisite: A crystal for contacting the ancient wisdom of Atlantis and Lemuria, Atlantisite teaches how to use your power wisely this time around.

Vibration: High.

Healing Qualities: Atlantisite is beneficial for cellular memory and stress reduction.

Aventurine: Aventurine links to the devic kingdom and is helpful for earth-healing. It reinforces leadership qualities and promotes compassionate understanding.

Vibration: Earthy.

Healing Qualities: Aventurine promotes well-being. It balances male/female energies and encourages regeneration of the heart.

Bloodstone: A major physical healing stone, Bloodstone was historically used to direct magical and spiritual rituals. It keeps out undesirable influences and heals the ancestral line.

Vibration: Earthy.

Healing Qualities: Stimulates the immune, circulation, and filtration systems. Bloodstone benefits blood-rich organs.

Charoite: Charoite is a stone that links to Chiron, the wounded healer archetype. This crystal has powerful transformative properties and brings the higher self into everyday reality. It assists anyone who is driven by other people's thoughts and programs rather than their own.

Vibration: Earthy and high.

Healing qualities: Charoite brings about profound physical and emotional healing.

Chrysocolla: A tranquil, sustaining stone, Chrysocolla assists meditation and spiritual communication. It helps you to accept with serenity anything that cannot be changed.

Vibration: Earthy or high depending on crystalline quality.

Healing Qualities: Chrysocolla transmutes negative energy into healing and converts dis-ease to wellness. It reenergizes when you are exhausted, heals and integrates dualities.

Coralite: Coral is a living species that should never be harvested, as it is under threat. It should only be collected when detached from the reef. Coralite is rock created from ancient, compressed fossils. Protective Coralite connects to the natural world and the ancestral. It can be harnessed to the forces of nature for earth-healing and to receive profound wisdom from the ancestors and spiritual masters.

Vibration: Earthy.

Healing Qualities: Coralite offers emotional healing.

Fluorite: Highly protective on a psychic level, Fluorite assists in discerning when undesirable outside influences are at work, ensuring that only beings with your highest good in mind communicate. It is helpful for dissolving past-their-sell-by-date fixed thoughts or behavioral patterns.

Vibration: Earthy.

Healing Qualities: Fluorite is a powerful healing tool, dealing with infections and disorders. It cleanses, purifies, dispels, and reorganizes anything within the body that is not in perfect order.

Hematite: Powerfully protective and grounding, Hematite redresses imbalances and imparts courage. It assists with focus and insight. It is perfect for a dragon or healing skull.

Vibration: Earthy.

Healing Qualities: Hematite restores, strengthens, and regulates the blood supply. The stone draws heat from the body.

Howlite: Often found dyed in garish colors, the underlying energy of Howlite is soft and gentle. It opens your attunement to the higher spiritual realms and assists communication.

Vibration: Earthy.

Healing Qualities: Howlite calms turbulent emotions, especially those that have past life causes. It releases the cords that tie old emotions to present life triggers.

Jade: Jade symbolizes wisdom. It promotes self-sufficiency. A protective stone, it encourages you to become who you truly are.

Vibration: Earthy.

Healing properties: Psychologically, Jade stabilizes the personality and integrates the mind with the body. It releases negative thoughts and soothes the mind.

Jasper: All the Jaspers are powerfully protective and nurturing. They facilitate shamanic journeying and accessing universal wisdom. Jasper aligns the chakras and is used in chakra layouts. The particular type of Jasper imparts subtle differences to the skull.

Vibration: Earthy to high according to type, but all ground the energy for healing.

Healing qualities: According to the specific type of Jasper (see *The Crystal Bibles*).

Labradorite: Labradorite aligns the physical and etheric bodies and accesses spiritual purpose. It raises consciousness and grounds spiritual energies into the physical body. This crystal creates an interface through which you interact with the unseen worlds. Labradorite skulls are occupied by beings with great spiritual wisdom.

Vibration: High.

Healing Qualities: Psychologically, Labradorite banishes fears, insecurities, and the psychic debris from previous disappointments, including past lives. It removes other people's projections, including thought forms that have hooked into the aura.

Lapis Lazuli: Lapis Lazuli enables you to safely connect to higher spiritual dimensions and spirit guardians. It is excellent for dealing with pain on any level.

Vibration: High.

Healing Qualities: A stone of transformation, Lapis Lazuli prepares body and soul for the assimilation of higher consciousness.

Malachite: This powerful stone rapidly brings hidden issues to the surface. It provides deep insights into the causes of behavior and stimulates suppressed memories. It needs to connect to a wise crystal mentor who advises on how to transform and heal such issues. It is not a skull for the fainthearted, but is perfect for an experienced emotional healer.

Vibration: Earthy and deep.

Healing Qualities: Malachite is an extremely versatile healing stone best used by an experienced therapist. Releasing psychosomatic causes, it realigns DNA and cellular structure, and enhances the immune system.

Mangano Calcite: This crystal stimulates the higher heart chakras, integrating universal love and understanding.

Vibration: High.

Healing Qualities: Mangano Calcite is particularly useful for heart and emotional healing.

Merlinite: Blending intuition and the intellect, magical and mystical Merlinite holds the combined knowledge of shamans, alchemists, magician-priests, and other workers of magic. Its dual coloring integrates spiritual and earthly vibrations. The stone supports during shamanic practices or magical ritual. A Merlinite skull assists in reading the Akashic Record, inducing travel into past or future lives to heal blockages and gain insight.

Vibration: Deep and high.

Healing Qualities: Merlinite is useful for past life healing and to bring harmony into the present life. It balances yin-yang and masculine and feminine energies, conscious and subconscious, intellect and intuition.

Morganite: A Pink Beryl, Morganite is a heart stone of great power and beauty. It helps people speak what was formerly unspeakable, holding the etheric body stable while psychosomatic patterns are dissolved. Morganite clears victim mentality and opens the heart to receive unconditional love. It dissolves unconscious blocks to healing and transformation, opening the way to spiritual advancement.

Vibration: High.

Healing Qualities: Morganite treats stress and stress-related illness.

Obsidian: Bringing hidden toxicity to the surface for transformation, natural Obsidian needs a strong mentor-being who advises on the best way to deal with this. The different colors and forms each subtly influence how a skull operates. The man-made glass blue and green Obsidian skulls have low underlying crystal resonance and provide a perfect home for a star being or other mentor. Care must be taken that such a being has your highest good in mind as Black Obsidian in particular may attract a less than desirable being.

Vibration: Earthy or neutral according to type.

Healing Qualities: Obsidian's greatest gift is insight into the cause of dis-ease. It assists the digestion of anything that is hard to accept. The natural form detoxifies and dissolves blockages and tension in the physical and subtle bodies.

Opalite: A synthetic material, milky Opalite is used to enhance spiritual communication, link to the higher self, and open the third eye. It brings peace and calm to any situation. As there is little underlying crystal resonance, it provides an energetically clear space for a mentor to take up residence.

Vibration: Neutral.

Healing Qualities: As a manufactured stone, Opalite has few natural healing qualities although it is said to stabilize mood swings.

Petalite: This is the perfect home for an angelic mentor or higher being. It helps you to raise your vibration to receive downloads of higher frequency information.

Vibration: Extremely high.

Healing Qualities: Petalite constantly energizes and activates all the energy centers of the body. It enhances and energizes the environment.

Petrified Wood: An excellent home for an earth-healer being, Petrified Wood assists with survival, renewal, and regeneration. It is the perfect stone for living in harmony with the cycles of nature and the seasons, and is particularly helpful for anyone who has been uprooted and needs to find their inner home.

Vibration: Earthy.

Healing Qualities: Petrified Wood is a useful emotional healer, especially if the cause is past life based. It assists regression to understand and release the root of a problem and then assists in instilling a new pattern.

Pietersite: Linking everyday consciousness to higher awareness, Pietersite facilitates reading the Akashic Record.

Vibration: Earthy.

Healing Qualities: Pietersite stimulates the pituitary gland, balancing the endocrine system and the production of hormones. It clears dis-ease caused by exhaustion in those who have no time to rest.

Preseli Bluestone: Accessing ancient Celtic wisdom, Merlin magic, and earth-healing, Preseli Bluestone facilitates shamanic journeying and attracts shaman mentors. It is the ideal skull for an earth-healer mentor or for those working with herbal medicine.

Vibration: Earthy and high.

Healing Qualities: Preseli Bluestone has a benign effect on the throat and the immune system, bringing the body's energies into balance.

Rhodochrosite: Rhodochrosite expands consciousness and integrates it into the everyday. A soulmate stone, it houses a mentor who is a long-term soul companion or twinflame. However, Rhodochrosite insists you face the truth about yourself and other people without excuses or evasions, but with loving awareness. This stone assists with diagnosis, so it is the perfect home for a healing guide.

Vibration: Earthy and high.

Healing Qualities: Rhodochrosite clears the solar plexus and base chakras.

Rhodonite: Rhodonite encourages the brotherhood of humanity. As the crystal assists in seeing both sides of the picture, it offers wise advice and assists in healing the trauma of abuse in this or other lives.

Vibration: Earthy.

Healing Qualities: This stone of emotional balance heals physical and soul shock and trauma.

Ruby in Zoisite: Ruby in Zoisite is a combination stone that activates the crown chakra, creating an altered state of consciousness. It also facilitates access of soul memory and spiritual learning. This stone heals heartbreak and past life pain and is the perfect crystal to house a guide who assists with transitions and grief counseling.

Vibration: Earthy and high.

Healing Qualities: Ruby in Zoisite powerfully amplifies the biomagnetic field around the body. It is extremely helpful in soul healing and in past life work.

Sodalite: Uniting the logical brain with the intuitive mind and bringing information from the higher mind down to Earth, Sodalite opens the third eye. It makes you more receptive to information a crystal mentor wishes to pass on to you. The stone encourages you to be true to yourself and your ideals.

Vibration: Earthy and high.

Healing Qualities: Sodalite balances the metabolism. It instills emotional balance and calms panic attacks, releasing the core fears, phobias, guilt, and control mechanisms that hold you back from being who you truly are.

Sugilite: Sugilite teaches how to live from your own truth and a loving heart. Sugilite heals shocks to the soul and is perfect for lightworkers who find the energy of the Earth too dense and need support.

Vibration: Earthy and high.

Healing Qualities: This crystal is excellent for anyone who has any kind of brain disorganization and needs to repattern on a physical or psychic level.

Tiger's Eye: Tiger's Eye is a grounded, energetic stone that assists in recognizing what you really need for your spiritual growth. It heals issues around self-worth and self-criticism, helping you to feel worthy of an evolved crystal mentor without bringing in pride or the ego. It assists in collecting scattered information to make a coherent whole. The different colors subtly amend the crystal's properties.

Vibration: Earthy and high.

Healing Qualities: Tiger's Eye integrates the brain hemispheres and enhances practical perception.

Tourmaline: The Tourmaline family of crystals are shamanic stones with multidimensional links. Protectors and purifiers, they disperse negative energy and ground spiritual energy. They have a strong affinity with the devic kingdom and so assist with earth-healing. Each color and type has an energetic connection with a particular chakra. Some, such as Watermelon, Indicolite, and Paraiba, have exceedingly fine vibrations and attract powerful spiritual mentors.

Vibration: Earthy and high, according to type.

Healing Qualities: Tourmaline enhances energy flow, making it an excellent stone for removal of blockages. Each of the different colors of Tourmaline has its own specific healing ability (see *The Crystal Bibles*).

Turquoise: Turquoise helps you to attune to the crystal mentors and wise beings who wish to communicate with you. It enhances your intuition and makes you more able to channel spiritual information from the highest sources. Useful if you tend to sabotage yourself, it assists in creative problem solving, making it the perfect home for a guidance mentor.

Vibration: Earthy and high.

Healing Qualities: Turquoise strengthens the meridians of the body and subtle energy fields. It enhances the physical and psychic immune systems and regenerates tissue.

Notes

INTRODUCING THE CRYSTAL SKULLS
1 See Resources for details of Petaltone Essences.

CHAPTER 1
1 Jaap Van Etten, PhD, *Crystal Skulls Interacting with a Phenomenon.*

2 *http://www.world-mysteries.com/sar_6_1.htm.*

3 *http://humansarefree.com/2014/05/the-history-of-crystal-skulls-and-their .html.*

4 See *http://crystal-skulls-mayan.com/* for the story of their discovery and the claims made for this pair of skulls.

5 Chris Morton and Cery Louise Thomas, *Mystery of the Crystal Skulls,* (London: Thorsons Publishing, 1998).

6 *http://medcell.med.yale.edu/cgi-bin/keyword.cgi?keyword=calcium%20 hydroxyapatite.*

Bocchi, Giancarlo; Valdre, Giovanni; Valdre, Giovanni (1993). "Physical, chemical, and mineralogical characterization of carbonate-hydroxyapatite concretions of the human pineal gland." *Journal of Inorganic Biochemistry* 49 (3): 209–20.

Baconnier, Simon; Lang, Sidney B.; Polomska, Maria; Hilczer, Bozena; Berkovic, Garry; Meshulam, Guilia (2002). "Calcite microcrystals in the pineal gland of the human brain: First physical and chemical studies." *Bioelectromagnetics* 23 (7): 488–95.

7 *www.wired.com/2014/10/future-of-artificial-intelligence/.*

CHAPTER 2

1 Marjan C. Meijer, *https://sites.google.com/site/mcmlove/crystalskulls3joky vandieten.*

2 *http://www.britishmuseum.org/explore/highlights/articles/s/studying_two_crystal_skulls.aspx.*

3 See interview with Nick Nocerino on *https://www.youtube.com/watch? v=51M_1–gVN4.*

4 See *http://www.strangemag.com/crystalskull/crystalskull.html,* which contains extensive references for the material perused. Note: every effort has been made to contact the website for permission to quote but so far to no avail.

5 Ibid.

6 Ibid.

7 Margaret Sax, Jane MacLaren Walsh, Ian C. Freestone, Andrew H. Rankin, Nigel D. Meeks, "The origin of two purportedly pre-Columbian Mexican crystal skulls," *Journal of Archaeological Science* 35, no. 10 (2008): 2751–2760.

Jane MacLaren Walsh, "What is Real? A New Look at PreColumbian Mesoamerican Collections," *AnthroNotes: Museum of Natural History Publication for Educators* 26, no. 1 (2005): 1–7, 17–19.

Jane MacLaren Walsh, "Legend of the Crystal Skulls," *Archaeology* 61, no. 3 (2008): 36–41.

8 Jane MacLaren Walsh, "Legend of the Crystal Skulls," *Archaeology* 61, no. 3 (2008): 36–41.

See *http://theappendix.net/issues/2013/4/the-fourth-skull-a-tale-of-authenticity-and-fraud* for the detailed story of Eugene Boban.

9 "Crystal skull," the Skeptics Dictionary. *http://skepdic.com/crystalskull .html.*

10 Jane MacLaren Walsh, "Under the microscope," *http://archive.archaeology .org/online/features/mitchell_hedges/microscope.html.*

11 *http://www.philipcoppens.com/mitchellhedges_origin.html.*

12 See Philip Coppens' "The Crystal Skull: A New Understanding" at *https://www.youtube.com/watch?v=t0hhnijMO0U.*

13 This passage by F. A. Mitchell-Hedges is taken from Phillip Coppens' website (*http://www.philipcoppens.com/mitchellhedges_origin.html*) and does

not provide a reference as to the original book page. It has not been possible as yet to verify the passage or to obtain permission for use. The passage is, however, cited in a Wikipedia article as appearing in Joe Nickell's *Adventures in Paranormal Investigation*. (Lexington: University Press of Kentucky, 2007), 69. The article by Philip Coppens appeared in *Nexus Magazine,* June/July 2008, 15, and as a two-part article in *Legendary Times* 9, no. 3/4 and 10, no. 1/2.

14 *http://www.britishmuseum.org/research/news/studying_the_crystal_skull .aspx.* The museum cites G. F. Kunz *Gems and Precious Stones of North America* (New York, 1890), 285–286.

15 Paul Rincon, *http://news.bbc.co.uk/go/pr/fr/-/1/hi/sci/tech/7414637.stm.*

16 N Charles C. Pelton, *Atlantis Rising* 10, (1997). Note: although this article appears in many sites on the Internet, it has not been possible to find any original source material from Pelton.

17 C. O'Brien, *The Mysterious Valley* (New York: St. Martin's Press, 1996), 288–294.

18 C. O'Brien, *Enter the Valley* (New York: St. Martin's Press, 1999), 251–254.

19 You can read this account for yourself on "Crystal Skulls 101," *http:// ericinmiami.blogspot.co.uk/.* It includes an account of sitting with the skulls Max and Einstein in addition to the images.

20 Michael E. Smith, *http://publishingarchaeology.blogspot.co.uk/2008/05/ blog-post.html.*

Michael E. Smith, "Aztec Materials in Museum Collections: Some Frustrations of a Field Archaeologist," *Nahua Newsletter* 38: 21–28.

https://en.wikipedia.org/wiki/Crystal_skull#cite_note-16.

CHAPTER 3

1 The Göbekli Tepe skull is at *https://www.iiconservation.org/node/4725.*

2 Alfonso Caso cited in Leopoldo Castedo's *A History of Latin American Art and Architecture* (London: Pall Mall Press, 1969).

3 Ibid., 46.

4 The skull was specifically from the Monte Alban Tomb 7 Museum, *www.paleodontology.com, Bulletin of the International Association for Paleodontology* 1, no. 2 (2007): 9–25, *https://scholar.google.co.uk/scholar?q=jade+ skulls&btnG=&hl=en&as_sdt=1%2C5.*

5   Donald A. Proulx, "Ritual Uses of Trophy Heads in Ancient Nasca Society," in *Ritual Sacrifice in Ancient Peru,* edited by Elizabeth Benson and Anita Cook (Austin: University of Texas Press, 2001): 119–136.

6   Patricia Mercier, *Crystal Skulls & the Enigma of Time* (London: Watkins Publishing, 2011).

7   Ibid.

8   See *http://magiedubouddha.com/p_tib-os1-intl.php* for a comprehensive survey of skull use around the world.

CHAPTER 4

1   *http://www.utexas.edu/features/2006/muertos/.*

2   *https://www.youtube.com/watch?v=51M_1-gVN4.*

3   *https://hiddenlighthouse.wordpress.com/category/crystal-skulls/.*

4   Keith Fauscett, *Chasing the Wind II: Return of the Crystal Skulls* (*Lulu.com,* 2009), 103.

It is unclear whether this book purports to be nonfiction as it reads more like illustrated fiction.

5   This information arises from my master's dissertation research, which was too extensive to quote as source material here. However, an extensive summary and bibliography of the idea of the crystalline spheres can be found on *https://en.wikipedia.org/wiki/Celestial_spheres.*

6   For a further exposition of the use of crystals in Atlantis, see James Tyberon's Metatron channeling on *http://www.thenewearth.org/The%20 Fall%20of%20Atlantis.html.*

CHAPTER 5

1   There is an interview with Nick Nocerino on *https://www.youtube.com/ watch?v=51M_1-gVN4* describing the ancient history of the Earth, its evolution, and interaction with UFOs.

CHAPTER 6

1   N Charles C. Pelton, *Atlantis Rising* 10 (1997).

2   See *http://www.crystalskulls.com/michele-nocerino.html.* And see the interview with Nick Nocerino on *https://www.youtube.com/watch?v=51M_1–gVN4* regarding the Mitchell-Hedges skull and scrying. The interview is an interesting example of skull mythology in action.

3 *https://jhaines6.wordpress.com/2011/11/03/.*

4 See *http://theothersidepress.com/635-635.*

5 *https://jhaines6.wordpress.com/2011/11/03/.*

6 *http://newrealities.com/index.php/articles-on-shamanism/item/1708-it-was-written-in-time-by-humbatz-men-mayan-daykeeper.*

7 *https://jhaines6.wordpress.com/2011/11/03/we-know-it%E2%80%99s-the-right-time-because-the-skulls-are-here-humbatz-men-monday-october-31-2011/.*

CHAPTER 7

1 *http://www.marythunder.com/CrystalSkulls/MaxTheCrystalSkull/MaxThe CrystalSkullMessage.htm.*

2 *http://www.pymander.com.*

CHAPTER 8

1 David A. Williams, Perren Professor of Astronomy, "Ashes to Ashes, Dust to Dust," *Oxford Journals, Science & Mathematics, Astronomy & Geophysics* 41, no. 3. 3.8–3.15. *http://astrogeo.oxfordjournals.org/content/41/3/3.8.full.*

2 If you doubt that multiverses or parallel realities exist, take a look at *http://themindunleashed.org/2014/01/parallel-worlds-exist-will-soon-testable-expert-says.html.*

3 *http://www.pymander.com.*

4 This appears all over the Internet and it's difficult to track down the primary source. See, for instance, *http://www.world-mysteries.com/sar_6_1.htm.*

CHAPTER 11

1 Jaap van Etten, *Crystal Skulls: Expand Your Consciousness* (Flagstaff, Arizona: Light Technology Publishing, 2013).

Jaap van Etten, *Crystal Skulls: Interacting with a Phenomenon* (Flagstaff, Arizona: Light Technology Publishing, 2007).

2 Frank Dorland on *http://www.strangemag.com/crystalskull/crystaldorland .html.*

CHAPTER 14

1 My thanks to Alphedia Arara for this information. Alphedia can be contacted at *www.elementalbeings.co.uk* or *www.facebook.co.uk/alphediaelemental beings.com.*

GLOSSARY

1 Tia Ghose, "Facts About Pangaea, Ancient Supercontinent," *http://www.livescience.com/38218-facts-about-pangaea.html.*

Glossary

Akashic Record. A subtle record of everything that has happened or could happen throughout all time frames, dimensions, and all universes.

Ancestral line. "The family tree." The ancestral line carries not only physical DNA but also attitudes, feelings, and emotions that affected the ancestors and that carry over to the descendants.

Aura/biomagnetic field. A subtle but measurable bioenergetic field that surrounds the physical body for some distance.

Chakra. An energy portal linking the physical body, the aura, and the multidimensional levels of being. A chakra mediates energy reaching the physical body and links to various organs of the body.

Consciousness. Consciousness is far more than just the brain or the mind. It is more than awareness of one's own existence, sensations, thoughts, and surroundings. Consciousness is boundless and interpenetrates and underpins everything. It is able to take individual form or spread into a vast cosmic field.

Crystal matrix. The crystalline structure or atomic net of a particular crystal.

Crystal skull conclave. A unified consciousness that resides within and beyond the crystal skulls. It may be experienced as individual skulls coming together as a council or as an energy field.

Dis-ease. A state resulting from physical imbalances, blocked feelings, suppressed emotions, and negative thinking which, if not reversed, leads to illness.

Earth-healing. Restoring balance and energetic well-being to Earth.

Earth star. A chakra beneath the feet that keeps you anchored in incarnation and connected to the planet.

Entrain. Two energies coming into harmony. Usually the larger force field entrains the smaller, but as the crystal frequency is more pure, it can entrain and return to harmony a larger field.

Etheric realms. The planes of existence closest to Earth in vibration. The lower etheric realm is the abode of unevolved and mischievous spirits.

Gaia gateway. A chakra beneath the feet that links the physical body and the soul to the planet and to Mother Earth. The chakra may be located two or three feet below the ground or deeper into the Earth itself, sometimes as deep as the mantle interface.

Healing. Restoring optimum balance to a body and clearing energetic blockages. It does not imply a cure.

Inclusions/occlusions. Natural features within an otherwise clear crystal such as swirls, phantoms, and inner crystals. The inclusions may be of a different crystal material.

Mentor being. A spirit or being who is not incarnated into a physical body and who, therefore, sees into past, present, and future to offer wise advice and counseling.

Meridian. Lines around the human or planetary body that convey energy and Qi (life force).

Multidimensions of consciousness. Subtle vibrational levels that encompass far more than the three-dimensional universe of time, space, and distance.

Multiverses. Multiple universes existing side by side.

Pangaea. A large landmass that existed in early geologic times, surrounded by one ocean. As part of the continuing process of creation, it formed from other landmasses approximately three hundred million years ago, and began to break apart about 175 million years ago into new continents, a process that continued over the next few million years until the present-day seven continents were formed. "This is what's driven the entire evolution of the planet through time. This is the major backbeat of the planet," said Brendan Murphy, a geology professor at the St. Francis Xavier University in Antigonish, Nova Scotia.[1] This is why crystals in one continent are energetically connected to those in another. Once upon a time they were one giant mass.

Piezoelectric and pyroelectric. Pyroelectricity is the ability of certain mineral crystals to generate an electrical charge when they are heated or cooled. A very small change in temperature produces an effect. The positive and negative charges move to opposite ends of the crystal, which becomes polarized and produces a voltage. The piezoelectric effect is the generation of an electric voltage upon application of mechanical stress or pressure.

Resonance. The vibration given off by all living things and sentient beings.

Scrying. Using a crystal to see into the past, present, or future.

Shamanic otherworlds: Shamans view the world as consisting of the lower, middle, and upper worlds. The worlds each have a specific vibrational rate and contain particular information. The lower world houses nature spirits and power animals, plant spirit medicine, and of course crystals. The middle world is that of the everyday. The upper world is the home of spirit mentors and star beings and our higher selves. The worlds may roughly equate to the unconscious or subconscious, conscious and supraconscious states of being.

Skullkeeper. A caretaker who is responsible for the welfare and maintenance of a skull in addition to interacting with it.

Third eye. The brow chakra located between and just above the eyebrows. This is the chakra of inner and outer metaphysical vision.

Trance. An altered state of consciousness in which perception is widened and receptivity heightened.

Resources

Books by Judy Hall

The Crystal Bible (volumes 1–3)
Crystal Prescriptions (volumes 1–6)
Crystals and Sacred Sites
Earth Blessings
Encyclopedia of Crystals
Judy Hall's Book of Psychic Development
(Flying Horse Press, Bournemouth)
101 Power Crystals

Crystal Skull Internet Sales Sites

Angel Additions (*www.angeladditions.co.uk*): This site is run by my daughter Jeni Campbell and sells crystals and skulls specially attuned by me. Jeni is also the supplier of Celtic healer crystals from the Welsh crystal dragon mountain.

Aristia (*www.aristia.co.uk*): A UK-based company run by crystal expert Michael Eastwood selling high-quality, premium-grade humanoid skulls already imbued with crystal mentors, including high-grade Quartzes from Brazilian carvers. Skulls in more unusual materials are also available.

Crystal Skulls (*www.CrystalSkulls.com*): A large company based in the United States offering a wide range of grades and types of skulls activated by contact with the ancient Tibetan skull Amar and the Mayan Blue Jade skull Cana Ixim. The site is constantly updated with new information and the latest research.

KSC Crystals (*www.ksccrystals.com*): A UK-based company run by Keith Birch, who offers reasonably priced rudimentary and average-grade skulls on his website.

Mineralbiz (*www.mineralbiz.com*): A Chinese company that specializes in affordable humanoid, star being, and dragon skulls sold through eBay and other Internet sites. Rapid service. Skulls can also be custom-made to order.

Raven (*www.ravensroost.net* and *www.Etsy.com*): A United States–based company offering beautiful, high-quality, super-premium-grade one-off pieces carved in their studio in a variety of materials and shapes that include animal skulls as well as humanoid. Excellent service. There is an interesting record of a skull being transformed from a raw crystal to the finished product at *www.ravensroost.net/creation.htm.*

Skullis (*www.skullis.com*): A company based in China that uses master craftsmen and offers a wide range of skull types at reasonable prices. Pieces include humanoid, alien/star beings, animals, and birds. Skulls are sent quickly and efficiently, and they offer an advisory service. Their parent company *www.rikoo.com* also offers skillful carvings. Both companies have reputable eBay stores.

Skull Cleansing
and Reenergizing Essences

Clear2Light from *www.petaltone.co.uk* and *www.petaltoneusa.com* is an excellent crystal cleanser and available worldwide. Z14 clears fourteen layers of the etheric. Crystal Charge is also available from Petaltone. Email David Eastoe for details on his heavy-duty cleansing essences for undesirable entities: *eastoe@yahoo.com.*

Crystal Cleanser spray from the Crystal Balance Company (*www.crystalbalance.net*) and Crystal Recharge used with transmuting Violet Flame work wonders.

Greenman Tree Essences (*www.greenmanshop.co.uk*) also produces excellent essences that are available worldwide.

Contributors

Alphedia Arara
   www.dragonwisdomschool.org/author/alphedia
   https://www.facebook.com/groups/elementalbeings/
   www.alphedia.co.uk
   www.elementalbeings.co.uk/

Terrie Birch
   www.astrologywise.co.uk, astrological readings and workshops

Edwin Courtney
   www.edwincourtenay.co.uk

Caroline Lake
   The Unexplained Show on *www.myspiritradio.com*

Emma Penman
   www.emmapenman.com, retreats, workshops, and private sessions

Jeni Powell

    The Crystal Balance Company, Energy Healing for Ultimate Wellbeing

    www.crystalbalance.co.uk

Susannah Rafaelle

    www.selfselectionforanimals.co.uk

Julia Surnina

    Confessions of a modern psychic blog, *www.juliasurnina.com*

Bibliography

Bryant, Alice, and Phyllis Galde. *The Message of the Crystal Skull.* St. Paul, Minnesota: Llewellyn's New Age Series, 1989.

Etten, Jaap van. *Crystal Skulls: Interacting with a Phenomenon.* Flagstaff, Arizona: Light Technology Publishing, 2007.

Fauscett, Keith. *Chasing the Wind II: Return of the Crystal Skulls.* Lulu.com, 2009.

Proulx, Donald A. "Ritual Uses of Trophy Heads in Ancient Nasca Society." In *Ritual Sacrifice in Ancient Peru.* Edited by Elizabeth Benson and Anita Cook. Austin: University of Texas Press, 2001.

Sax, Margaret, Jane M. Walsh, Ian C. Freestone, Andrew H. Rankin, and Nigel D. Meeks. "The origin of two purportedly pre-Columbian Mexican crystal skulls." *Journal of Archaeological Science* 35, no. 10 (2008): 2751–2760.

Walsh, Jane MacLaren. "What is Real? A New Look at PreColumbian Mesoamerican Collections." *AnthroNotes: Museum of Natural History Publication for Educators* 26, no. 1 (2005): 1–7, 17–19.

———. "Legend of the Crystal Skulls." *Archaeology* 61, no. 3 (2008): 36–41.

Also see the Notes section.

About the Author

Judy Hall is a successful Mind-Body-Spirit author of forty-nine books (translated into fifteen languages) including the best-selling *Crystal Bible* (volumes 1–3). Her specialities include past life readings and regression, soul healing, reincarnation, astrology and psychology, divination, and crystal lore. She has been a past-life therapist and karmic astrologer for over forty-five years. Judy is an internationally known author, psychic, healer, broadcaster and workshop leader. She has appeared four times on the *Watkins Review* list of the one hundred most spiritually influential authors this century and was *Kindred Spirit's* 2014 MBS (Mind, Body, Spirit) personality of the year.

A trained healer and counselor, Judy has been psychic all her life and has a wide experience of many systems of divination and natural healing methods. Judy has a BEd in Religious Studies with an extensive knowledge of world religions and mythology and an MA in Cultural Astronomy and Astrology at Bath Spa University. Her mentor was Christine Hartley (Dion Fortune's metaphysical colleague and literary agent). She runs crystal, past life, astrological, and creative writing courses. Judy has conducted workshops around the world and has made numerous visits to Egypt, the subject of her novel *Torn Clouds*. For more information, see *www.judyhall.co.uk* and Crystal Judy Hall and The Crystal Bible Facebook pages.

To Our Readers

Weiser Books, an imprint of Red Wheel/Weiser, publishes books across the entire spectrum of occult, esoteric, speculative, and New Age subjects. Our mission is to publish quality books that will make a difference in people's lives without advocating any one particular path or field of study. We value the integrity, originality, and depth of knowledge of our authors.

Our readers are our most important resource, and we appreciate your input, suggestions, and ideas about what you would like to see published.

Visit our website at *www.redwheelweiser.com* to learn about our upcoming books and free downloads, and be sure to go to *www.redwheelweiser.com/newsletter* to sign up for newsletters and exclusive offers.

You can also contact us at *info@rwwbooks.com* or at

Red Wheel/Weiser, LLC
665 Third Street, Suite 400
San Francisco, CA 94107